The authors clearly describe how college athletics brings a unique set of challenges to an already tumultuous developmental stage of life. The literature review coupled with practical suggestions to assist with the academic, athletic, and personal transitions makes this an ideal textbook for an adjustment to college course. This book is a must-have resource for anyone working directly with college student-athletes.

Carmen Tebbe Priebe, Ph.D.
Psychologist
University of Oklahoma Athletics Department

Overall I think *Winning at the College Level* definitely touches on all of the issues, topics and concerns that student-athletes go through from depression to talking to an instructor. This book would be a great tool to use in freshmen orientation classes for student-athletes because of the encompassing topics and the interactive workbook. It is a very good resource for both student-athletes and academic support units.

Megan Albidrez, Associate Director
Academic Support Program for Student Athletes
North Carolina State University

Dr. Tyrance and Dr. NiiLampti both have first-hand knowledge of what it takes to succeed as a student-athlete. Both also have worked extensively with student-athletes in various roles and at multiple levels. Their understanding of today's student-athlete is evident throughout the book. This is the rare book that includes sound advice on virtually all types of challenges, issues and opportunities that our student-athletes face today. As an instructor I love the end of section reflections and the various worksheets which are ready for classroom use.

Mark Verburg, Associate Director & Tutor Coordinator
Athletics Academic Center
University of North Carolina at Charlotte

Winning at the College Level is a road map for all first-year student-athletes. This book helps student-athletes identify campus resources, effectively manage their time and provides them with the tools and confidence to reach their personnel and professional goals. This book takes a holistic approach in developing student-athletes to be leaders on their teams, within the Athletic Department and on campus. I truly believe this book will enhance the student-athlete experience.

Jason Cable, Associate Athletic Director
Alcorn State University

Winning at the College Level: Thriving as a First-Year Student-Athlete is an excellent and well-written manual for any incoming collegiate student-athlete. The practical and applied nature of this book provides student-athletes, coaches, and staff with great "tools" to enhance the adjustment success for any first year student-athlete. Shaun and Nyaka have created a unique and "user-friendly" guide for readers and instructors; this text can be easily incorporated into current transitional classes, workshops, and academic services for the collegiate student-athlete.

Chris Carr, Ph.D.
rt & Performance Psychologist
t. Vincent Sports Performance

WINNING AT THE COLLEGE LEVEL:

THRIVING AS A FIRST-YEAR STUDENT-ATHLETE

By

Shaun Tyrance, Ph.D.

&

Nyaka NiiLampti, Ph.D.

Winning at the College Level:
Thriving as a First-Year Student-Athlete

Hero House Publishing
6060 Piedmont Row Drive South
Suite 120
Charlotte, NC 28287
www.herohousepublishing.com

Edited by Sara Caitlyn Deal; Cover design by Ben Berg; Text design by Sara Caitlyn Deal

---

Winning at the college level: thriving as a first–year student-athlete / Tyrance, S. & NiiLampti, N.

ISBN-13: 978-0-615-41350-1

FORWARD

Every year, for nearly twenty years, I have had the pleasure of working with a new class of first-year student-athletes as they navigate the challenges of a new campus community. Because each of them brings their own individual history, values, and perspective to the equation, and because every campus has it's own unique environment, it is impossible to predict who will struggle to succeed. I have seen student-athletes with terrific transcripts, test scores, and grade point averages struggle to survive their first year for reasons that have nothing to do with academic preparation. Conversely, I have seen just as many students with little or no preparation experience incredible success in their first year.

Despite the incalculable variables individuals and institutions bring to the equation for success, it still amazes me how constant the solution remains. No matter what circumstances led you to your first-year, the fact is, there is a template for a successful transition, and Shaun and Nyaka have provided it in plain and relatable terms. *Winning at the College Level* reads like a clearly defined map identifying every challenge and opportunity first-year student-athletes will encounter along their journey. Whether you are a freshman right out of high school, a transfer student, an international student, a parent, a coach, or an academic advisor, you'll find helpful advice to navigate the obstacles to academic, athletic, social, and personal success.

Like Shaun and Nyaka, I was a student-athlete in college. I actually struggled through a first-year transition three times; once as a freshman and twice as a transfer. I learned the hard way that you have to leave your comfort zone to be successful and that you need other people to succeed. At the University of Georgia, we like to say that we put the first year first, because it establishes the foundation, or what we call the launching pad, for the future trajectory of each student-athlete.

I wish I had access to this text when I was a freshman and a transfer. I am certainly glad it's available to today's student-athletes! More than just a book that describes the campus landscape, this work blends relevant statistics and quotes from actual student-athletes with thoughtful discussion points and reflection questions. Used by an individual or applied in a classroom setting, the worksheets and activities provide readers with the knowledge of self that is absolutely critical to goal-setting and overcoming adversity along the path.

Ted White
Associate Athletic Director for Academic Services
University of Georgia

TABLE OF CONTENTS

INTRODUCTION

Welcome to college! You've officially made it. You have survived the stress of being a high school senior, you've successfully navigated the process of finding the right college for you, and you have walked across the graduation stage. Congratulations! Those are all very difficult tasks, and you should be proud of your accomplishments. You are one of the few privileged high school student-athletes to have the opportunity to play in college. According to recent National Collegiate Athletic Association (NCAA) stats, only between 3 and 11% of high school athletes in your sport get the chance to play on a college campus (Probability of Competing, 2013). In your new role as a college student-athlete, you will have the opportunity and pleasure to travel, meet new people, and experience competition at one of your sport's highest levels.

There are multiple benefits both on and off the field that accompany participating in collegiate athletics. Athletes who compete at this level have access to a high quality educational experience, state of the art training resources, chances for national and international travel, exposure to new cultures, and opportunities to develop skills that translate to life beyond college. Most importantly, athletes have a greater chance of attaining with a degree in comparison to other college students (NCAA, 2013). Your new life as a first-year college student-athlete has just begun. While the benefits are many, there are also many challenges inherent in your role as a college athlete. Not only do first-year student-athletes have to manage all that encompasses the completely unfamiliar environment of college, there are also new coaches and teammates to add to that adjustment. Some of you may also be experiencing other firsts—you may be the first in your family to attend college, or this may be the first time you have ever been away from home for an extended period of time. You may have left a small town where you have grown up surrounded by the same familiar faces, and everyone knows who you are. Or you may have spent the last 18 years of your life in a major city with millions of people, and are now living in a small town where not many people share your background or culture.

These are all variables that can impact how happy and successful you are during your first-year as a college athlete, as research indicates that students who are successful their first-year have a greater likelihood of returning and eventually graduating from college (Ishitani & DesJardins, 2002). Our goal is to help you persist through the ups and downs of college athletics and successfully manage the inevitable challenges in a way that results in a rewarding college experience and degree completion. While we know that many student-athletes enter college with the hope of playing professional sports, statistics published by the NCAA remind us that for the majority of sports there is a less than 2% chance of being drafted by a professional sports organization (Probability of Competing, 2013). This book was created to serve as a resource for first-year student-athletes looking to excel in their sport and in the classroom. The information included in this text is designed to guide you toward degree completion while simultaneously experiencing great athletic success. And since studies indicate that college graduates can earn more than a million dollars more than someone with a high school diploma over the course of their lifetime, we believe that successfully managing your first year of college puts you securely on that path (U.S. Department of Education, 2013).

> Almost 20% of upperclass student-athletes surveyed thought it was likely that they would play professional sports, and an additional 28% were not ruling it out as a possibility.

Although some universities suggest student-athletes are no different from the non-athlete students on campus, the truth is that student-athletes are part of a "special population" and are faced with the unique challenge of balancing academic requirements with the physically demanding and time draining schedule of college athletics. All first-year students (athletes and non-athletes) face a number of challenges that may contribute to adjustment difficulties. Specifically, first-year college students are required to adjust in two primary areas: academic and social. The struggle to navigate these two worlds is so demanding that recent studies indicate almost 35% of college students drop out between their first and second year (U.S. Department of Education, 2013). In addition to the social and academic demands that most first-year college students experience, student-athletes are faced with navigating the additional world of college athletics. As a result, your transition during this time may be more challenging than non-athletes. You will want to be strategic about how you negotiate your first year, and proactively manage each of the domains that pose a potential threat to your success on and off the field.

As former Division I student-athletes who have worked with thousands of college athletes as sport psychology consultants, this book is a result of discussions about our own first-year experiences, both on the field and in the classroom. We have both experienced interactions with other students (and sometimes faculty) who did not believe that student-athletes held as much value as non-athletes. We have personally experienced the challenges of balancing study sessions with sports practice, and sometimes missed out on opportunities to create informal relationships with faculty members. In addition to our own experiences, many of the college student-athletes we work with as clinicians, sport performance consultants, and faculty members have also had similar experiences. What has become evident is that several student-athletes continue to struggle in these areas and are unable to take full advantage of the opportunities associated with being a student-athlete. These missed opportunities can result in academic or athletic ineligibility, poor decision making, and in extreme cases, early dismissal or voluntary withdrawal. The continued struggles we witness among college athletes across the country indicate there is a strong need for additional support and resources.

As you begin and progress through your first year of college, you will undoubtedly encounter numerous experiences that could alter—positively or negatively—how successful you are in your sport or in the classroom. In fact, many universities have created courses for first-year student-athletes to assist you as you navigate this transition. We hope this text will serve as an additional resource for you and supplement transition courses that have been designed specifically to support your adjustment. As mentioned previously, statistics indicate that going from college athletics to professional or Olympic sports is highly unlikely; however, the possibility of this progression decreases—or becomes virtually impossible—if you are dismissed or leave prematurely (Probability of Competing, 2013). This book is structured to inform you, prepare you, and provide you with the tools you will need throughout your athletic and academic college career.

Winning at the College Level is different from any first-year transition book you will encounter, as it is written from a student-athlete's perspective. It presents a practical and straightforward approach to addressing the challenges and benefits of the first-year student-athlete experience. We understand that a successful student-athlete excels in both adjusting to the athletic demands of college sports and managing academics. It is with that balance in mind that this book has been structured. This book is divided into two major parts: Part I provides content rich information on the first-year transition for student-athletes, and Part II, the "College Survival Guide", is comprised of worksheets that allow student-athletes to learn useful skills that will enable them to discover themselves and develop the necessary tools that will be helpful in college and beyond.

> **"You've got to stay focused on what is important to you. And as a student-athlete, it should be student first and athlete second. Because when it comes down to it, that's why you're here. Don't forget why you're in college. You're in college to get an education."**
> *-Senior, Women's Basketball*

Part I is organized into three chapters structured around the central domains you, as a student-athlete, will navigate: athletic, academic, and social transitions. Each chapter will present information on several important topics within each domain, pointers that provide insight into the most common concerns student-athletes have expressed in each area, and suggestions to aid in successfully navigating them. While each of these chapters covers information specific to the primary domain, there are three additional elements that we found important to address in each chapter: mental health issues within student-athlete populations and the unique experiences of international and transfer student-athletes.

Studies tell us that although the benefits of participating in sports are countless, student-athletes often struggle with some mental health issues at a higher rate than non-athletes, particularly depression, anxiety, and eating disorders (Watson & Kissinger, 2007; Storch, Storch, Killiany, & Roberti, 2005; Pinkerton, Hinz & Barrow, 1989). While we do not often discuss these issues among athletes, if signs and symptoms of these challenges are ignored, they can negatively impact performance and if continually left untreated, can have life-long consequences. From a developmental perspective, we know that college age is the time at which many mental health issues begin to present themselves (Burke, Burke, Regier & Rae, 1990; Kessler, Berglund, Demler, Jin, Merikangas & Walters, 2005). Additionally, the stressors associated with the process of navigating such a significant transition can increase the likelihood of onset of emotional difficulties. There is often reluctance among student-athletes around seeking support or asking for help, especially for concerns related to mental health issues (Watson, 2005; Martin, Wrisberg, & Lousbury, 1996). This text provides information about the most common mental health issues experienced by student-athletes, as well as signs and symptoms to help you recognize when there may be need for concern. The information provided in each chapter is based on the criteria listed in the most commonly used mental health diagnostic manual (DSM-5; American Psychiatric Association, 2013). We would encourage you to seek support from a licensed mental health professional, your athletic department sport psychologist, or the university counseling center if you recognize these symptoms either in friends, teammates, or yourself.

Each chapter also includes a section that speaks specifically to experiences of international and transfer student-athletes, who again, are required to navigate more responsibilities than non-athlete students in both populations. While many of the experiences of these two groups of student-athletes will parallel those of other first-year student-athletes, there are some areas in which their experiences will differ. For example, transfer students are at an advantage in many ways when compared to first-year athletes—they have already experienced the higher level of preparation and competition, the demands of balancing academics, sports, and social life, as well as the adjustment related to being away from home. While research indicates that student-athletes who transfer from junior colleges to four year institutions have a greater difficulty in making this adjustment, all transfer students will benefit from following the suggestions outlined in this text to ensure their academic, athletic and social success (McGuire, S.P. & Belcheir, M., 2013; Townsend & Wilson, 2008).

Though there are advantages, disadvantages are also possible—some transfer student-athletes may feel increased pressure to perform resulting from limited time to accomplish athletic and academic goals. Depending on previous experiences, some may have to unlearn bad habits or expectations, or may struggle to connect socially with team-mates, coaches, or faculty. International student-athletes may face challenges as a result of the cultural shifts between their home country and their new environment, including language, expectations, and building relationships. As a result, each chapter discusses additional challenges that these two populations may face and provides suggestions to assist them in navigating the concerns that may be specific to them.

Part II of this text is the College Survival Guide, a workbook intended to help you learn more about yourself in areas such as values, athletic identity, learning preferences, and study skills. The worksheets and activities in this section will guide you in developing skills in each of these areas and provide tools that we have learned are essential to success in higher education. We know that many students come to college lacking strong time management and study skills. Not only will the College Survival Guide support you as you learn many of these skills, it is also structured to allow you to learn about yourself as a student and as a person. For example, knowing

> "I probably made some of my lowest grades as a freshman because I was studying the same way I did in high school...and not working as hard, not reading the theory or reading the book as much or understanding the information. And not getting the help because I thought I could do it myself."
> *-Senior, Women's Cross Country*

your particular learning style—Are you auditory or visual? Do you learn by teaching or doing?—will help you both in the classroom and on the field. Surprisingly, many students do not learn this important information about themselves until later in their college career. This book will allow you to gain this knowledge in your first-year and therefore you will be able to maximize your potential from the beginning.

This comprehensive resource guide is based on surveys, interviews, and focus groups we conducted with upper class student-athletes to gain insight into their first-year experiences. You will see their voices and suggestions woven throughout the book. Each of the first three chapters concludes with discussion questions that will help generate classroom dialogue as well as journal space for you to jot down your thoughts or additional questions.

The purpose of this text is to ease your transition into higher education; to help you balance your academic, athletic, and social demands and increase your ability to have both a fulfilling athletic career and earn a college degree. It is our hope that as you work your way through this book, you will find yourself learning these skills and applying the techniques both in the classroom and on the field. We believe (and the research indicates) that if you put these skills into practice, you will find some aspects of your first year less overwhelming and increase your chances of success. As two individuals who have gone from student-athletes in college to working with student-athletes in our post-collegiate lives, our goal is to help you make your college experience and beyond enjoyable and successful!

Part I: The Student-Athlete Transition

Chapter 1: The Academic Transition

Chapter 2: The Athletic Transition

Chapter 3: The Social/Cultural Transition

Chapter 1:
The Academic
Transition

One of the most significant challenges all first-year students will face is the higher level of academic rigor that exists at the collegiate level. All students must contend with increased levels of academic pressure and the elevated expectations that college professors have for their students. Couple this greater academic demand with the increased amount of personal freedom students have and the college classroom can be a daunting place for first-year students. While it can be easy to allow your athletic responsibilities (practice, rehab, and competition) to interfere with your studies, it's important to keep in mind that the term *student-athlete* is stressed for a reason. For many of you, it may be the first time you have to organize your schedule and manage your time by yourself. It may be the first time you're handed a syllabus and simply told when assignments are due, meaning it is your responsibility to make sure that work is completed on time and you are adequately prepared for quizzes and exams. While there are a number of factors that contribute to the academic experience of student-athletes, you can prepare yourself by knowing what to expect and setting yourself up for success from the very beginning.

> "I think it's very important for people to know that high school is a lot easier than college. If I knew how hard college was going to be, I would have done a lot better in high school. Because you don't get to hand work in late. Teachers expect you to read the syllabus, and to know what's going on. You need to put in way more hours. You need to become the library's best friend. Especially during exams. And it's so much more demanding. Teachers expect more of you." -Sophomore, Men's Basketball

On some college campuses, student-athletes face various stereotypes when it comes to classroom performance. While these stereotypes are often inaccurate, they can nonetheless influence the perspective of your professors and your peers. Concern about those negative stereotypes may even impact your performance…both inside and outside the classroom (Yopyk, & Prentince, 2005; Stone, Harrison, & Mottley, 2012; Dee, 2014). It is important that you don't fall victim to these stereotypes! Prepare yourself for the academic challenge, and attack it with the same vigor and intensity that you do your sport. Remember, less than **two percent** of college student-athletes make it in professional sports (Probability of Competing, 2013). You are the one who suffers if you do not take advantage of your academic opportunity.

> 29% of upperclass student-athletes indicated that as freshmen, they did not participate in class discussions for fear of being judged because of their athletic status.

> "I've gotten the 'how are you possibly a physics major because athletes are stupid' thing so often that I think there's a general perception that most student athletes are of lower intelligence."-Senior, Women's Swimming

Academic Expectations

There are a few fundamental academic tasks that will require a greater level of attention than you may be used to. College courses are typically designed very differently from high school classes; they are structured to assess your ability to understand and apply learned information, rather than simply memorize and repeat facts. As a result, strong study skills, test taking knowledge, the ability to engage in critical thought, and the capability to express your views and understanding in writing are vital to your success. While you have done each of these to some degree in high school, college success requires you to bring these abilities to another level.

> 16% of upperclass student-athletes felt that their professors occasionally viewed them as "dumb jocks" during their first year.

One of the most effective ways to learn how to manage academic expectations is to develop a good relationship with your advisor. If you are lucky enough to have an advisor in your major and an advisor in the athletic department, make sure you connect with both individuals. Understand that each advisor is different; you will have to be a strong advocate for yourself to ensure you get the academic information needed to guarantee your overall success. Understand both the NCAA's and your institutions continuing eligibility requirements. There are a lot of rules (i.e. number of hours completed in each semester, percentage toward degree, total hours passed). Do not rely solely on your advisors, as they sometimes make mistakes. Take responsibility for your own success and don't put your athletic and academic career in the hands of others.

Writing Skills

Unfortunately, it is not uncommon for students—athletes and non-athletes—to enter college with limited experience and skills in formal writing. Most high school classes do not require extensive writing assignments where developing a thesis statement and integrating supporting ideas in a structured format are necessary (Mosley, 2006). As a result, many students have limited experiences organizing their thoughts in a coherent manner and putting them down on paper. Performing well in college courses will require you to express yourself clearly through writing, in papers as well as essay and short answer questions on exams. It is a common misperception that you are only graded on your writing abilities in your English class. Your Political Science professor is equally interested in your ability to clearly express your ideas on paper, and your grade will be impacted by that skill.

Writing effectively is often seen as an intimidating task to students of all academic backgrounds and strengths. While it can be a challenge to develop and strengthen this skill, it is not a challenge student-athletes need to embark upon alone. Almost all universities have an Academic Support Center of some kind that provides students with a variety of services to contribute to academic success. In some university athletic programs, there are academic support programs embedded within the department; and others may be a part of the larger university. Despite the location on campus, these centers typically have a resource that specifically focuses on providing writing support. Writing centers provide support for each component of the writing process, from idea generation and organization to proofreading and editing a final product. In most cases, using this resource is not a requirement, and unfortunately lots of students miss out on the opportunity to not only increase their grade on an individual assignment but also to further develop writing skills and improve future outcomes as well. Make sure you utilize this support!

In the College Survival Guide, Section 7 is dedicated to helping you develop your writing skills and manage the writing process. Worksheet 7.1 and the Writing Skills Tipsheet will be particularly useful for your early writing assignments, but will also provide writing support throughout your college experience. Worksheet 7.1 gives you a format to outline and structure writing assignments, while the Tipsheet highlights common writing errors to avoid. The Journaling worksheet in the stress management section (Section 10.3) can also be used to help further develop your writing skills.

Reflection Time:
- *What part of the writing process is the biggest challenge for you?*
- *What are factors that would prevent you from using the resources in the Academic Support Center?*

Study Skills

Another skill that is essential in college is your ability to take in information, take notes, and study effectively. First-year students often think they are well informed in this area, and find it surprising when they do not perform well on tests or exams. Effective test taking requires you to be well prepared, aware of what content needs to be studied, and knowledgeable about your most effective study method. It is important that you understand not everyone studies in the same manner; a method that may be effective for a roommate or teammate may not necessarily work for you. Additionally, your study approach may vary depending on the course, content, or type of exam or test.

> "In high school, I could just sit in class and daydream really, and not worry about the material being taught or anything like that. So then when I got here to college, I still kind of had that attitude. I'd just sit there and take a few notes, not really worry too much. And then I was realizing that my workload was too big when it was time for exams."
> *-Junior, Women's Field Hockey*

Successfully navigating your first year academically will require you to gain some awareness about the quality of your current study skills, and ways that you may need to strengthen these skills. For example, simply reading through your notes in preparation for an exam that is designed to assess your application of information (instead of simply defining terms) may not allow you to achieve the results you desire. Similarly, you may need to alter your current method of note taking. For some classes, taking notes during class based on what your professor discusses may be ample preparation for the exam. In other courses you will find that much of the exam is based on information you learn from reading the textbook and taking good notes, while in some classes you may find that exams are based on a combination of both. The College Survival Guide, will provide you with several tools that allow you to assess your skill set in this area and give you a few pointers that will enable you to be more successful.

Academic Integrity

Academic integrity covers a fairly wide range of concepts, including honor codes and plagiarism. This is a term that is being addressed more frequently in higher education today. Maintaining a certain standard and level of honesty in all course related activities is the foundation of academic integrity. While every institution varies in the level of emphasis they place on promoting this concept, students everywhere are held responsible for upholding academic integrity. What exactly does the term "academic integrity" mean? In brief, the word "integrity" speaks to honesty and the following of a high ethical and moral standard (Mish, 2004). Academic integrity means applying that same high ethical standard in and out of the classroom. The violation of academic integrity is most commonly associated with cheating and/or plagiarism, resulting in an unfair academic advantage over other students.

> 10% of upperclass student-athletes worried about being caught cheating or plagiarizing during their freshman year.

Studies have shown that anywhere between 50% and 90% of high school students admit to cheating in some form (Strom & Strom, 2007; Galloway, 2012; Bacha, Bahous & Nabhani, 2012). This could be anything from providing classmates information about what is on an upcoming exam, to circulating correct answers by Facebook or email, to using the Internet as a resource, or collaborating on assignments when it is not allowed. Many high school students feel that cheating is just "part of the culture," and often do not express feelings of guilt or wrong doing for their actions. Additionally, they feel there are limited consequences in the unlikely case they get caught. Some high school students admit that they have become so desensitized to cheating and academic dishonesty that they sometimes are able to convince themselves that they are not behaving immorally (Cheating Fact Sheet, 2013).

Making the transition from high school, where these behaviors may not come with a significant cost or consequence, into college, where expulsion or other serious punishments are a consequence of cheating, requires a very large shift in thinking. Many schools have a well-established Honor Code System that attaches a heavy penalty to acts of academic dishonesty. Unfortunately, at many institutions, student-athletes have a higher profile than their non-athletes counterparts and are sometimes held to a higher standard. As a result, they may be used as "the example" when rules are broken. Honor Code Systems vary by university; generally, they are used as a means of providing structure and formality around the theme of academic integrity that without clarification can be misinterpreted or misunderstood.

Honor Code Systems define what academic integrity means for that institution, describe the roles and responsibility of each student in upholding the honor code, explain the process that occurs when a violation occurs, and describe the range of consequences that may follow. Honor code violations can vary—they might include knowing that someone in your class has cheated or acted dishonestly and failing to inform your professor/faculty, or providing assistance to someone, despite knowing that assistance on a particular task is not allowed. More egregious acts would include actions such as copying a writing assignment straight from Wikipedia.

Many institutions have a committee that is tasked with the specific responsibility of listening to Honor Code violations and doling out consequences that are fair and equitable. For most institutions, the consequences for academic dishonesty can range from failing the assignment, to failing the course, to even expulsion. Needless to say, failing a course due to academic dishonesty can jeopardize your athletic eligibility. Therefore, it would be beneficial for you to know and understand your institution's academic integrity policy. Each professor may interpret the policy differently, but it is your responsibility to uphold your institution's policy and protect your academic and athletic eligibility. The following insert is an example of an institution's Honor Code. Note the clearly outlined descriptions of unacceptable behaviors for students. Again, each institution will have its own Honor Code policy or student code of conduct; be certain that you know what is expected at your university.

> *Each Davidson student is honor bound to refrain from stealing, lying about College business, and cheating on academic work. Stealing is the intentional taking of any property without right or permission. Lying is intentional misrepresentation of any form. Cheating is any practice, method, or assistance, whether explicitly forbidden or unmentioned, that involves any degree of dishonesty, fraud, or deceit. Cheating includes plagiarism, which is representing another's ideas or words as one's own. Additional guidelines for each class may be determined by its professor; each Davidson student is responsible for knowing and adhering to them. Each student is responsible for learning and observing appropriate documentation of another's work. Each Davidson student is honor bound to report immediately all violations of the Honor Code of which the student has first-hand knowledge; failure to do so is itself a violation of the Honor Code. All students, faculty, and other employees of Davidson College are responsible for familiarity with and support of the Honor Code. Any student, faculty member, administrative officer, employee, or guest of the College may charge a student with a violation of the Honor Code. Charges are presented to the Dean of Students and at the Dean's discretion must be signed. If the Dean determines that further proceedings are warranted by the Honor Council, he or she will prepare a formal charge. Hearings, administrative conferences and other proceedings regarding alleged violations of the Honor Code shall be conducted pursuant to the Code of Disciplinary Procedures.—Davidson College's Honor Code*

There are some simple ways to guarantee that you maintain academic integrity at all times and avoid the possible pitfalls that can come as a result of even inadvertent violations. The first suggestion would be to communicate with professors to ensure that your understanding of the assignment matches their intent. For example, *"Is collaboration acceptable?" "Is this an individual assignment?"* Ask questions if there is any lack of clarity around the rules. The second suggestion would be to make sure that you utilize the resources available to you at your institution. Many of you have access to academic support staff that can provide assistance with almost any questions you have regarding what is acceptable academically, and if those support staff aren't certain of the answer, they certainly know where to go to get the right answer. Ask questions. Seek feedback. Many students come to college with limited experiences writing papers and citing sources correctly. Use your campus Writing Center to ensure that your writing assignments include the necessary citations and avoid the possibility of plagiarism, particularly as this is often one of the most common Honor Code violations on college campuses.

Reflection Time:
- *Identify four actions that would be considered violations of your institution's honor code.*
- *What would be the procedure and/or consequences if you committed an honor code violation at your institution?*

Navigating the Classroom

For most of you, the largest classrooms you might have experienced have 35-40 students. For many college classes, particularly in the first two years, lecture halls hold upwards of 200 people. This typically means that attendance is not taken, distractions abound, and to your professor, you may be nothing more than a name on a sheet of paper. Resist the temptation to blend in among your peers, tucked away safely in a seat in the back of the class. While this action doesn't always result in poor academic performance, it is easier to become disengaged when you are so far away from the instructor. Keeping this in mind, it is essential to be actively engaged and to develop a relationship with your professors to increase your chance of success in large lecture classes.

52% of upperclass student–athletes reported that during their first year, they were intimidated to participate in class discussions due to large class size.

First, take note of the office hours of your professors or Teaching Assistants (TA's). Preferably after the first class or two, but definitely during the first week of class, approach your professor at the end of class or make the time to stop by their office. Introduce yourself and ask for their suggestions around how students can be successful in their class, share with your instructors that you are a student-athlete, and inform them—as early as possible—of the days when you will have to miss class or leave early due to a conflict with a competition. It will be extremely helpful if you have already consulted your athletic schedule and compared it to the class syllabus to identify potential scheduling conflicts. Some athletic departments provide official documentation or "travel letters" that inform your professors of class absences. You should also ask for suggestions about ways to make up the work or information you will miss during those days and times. While some professors may feel that missing class due to athletic commitments is unacceptable or annoying (unfortunately, some do feel this way), you can minimize negative impact by demonstrating your responsibility and communicating this concern as early as possible in the semester. Introducing yourself and interacting with your professors also moves you from being a name on a roster to someone they recognize both in class as well as when assignments are graded. Remember, professors are human, and they want their students to be successful. If you show them that you care and that you are willing to put forth the necessary effort to earn a good grade in their course, your chances of success increase exponentially.

Unfortunately, what often happens to first-year student-athletes (many first-year students—nonathletes included) is that they feel overwhelmed by the large class size and attempt to be as "invisible" as possible. They may automatically sit in the back of the class or in the last row, which makes it easier to become distracted by the many students in front of and around them, the thoughts about what they are going to do after class that day, or the leaves falling from the trees outside of the window! While you may not always notice the professor, keep in mind that the person in front of the class can always see you; they have a "bird's eye view" of the entire classroom. They notice students who are texting and constantly checking their smartphones, students surfing Facebook under the guise of using their laptop to take notes, students staring out of the window, and students who may be sleeping as a result of 7am practice or late night partying.

---

7 Ways to Navigate the Classroom

- Introduce yourself to the professor and/or TA.
- Compare your sport schedule to the class syllabus.
- Inform your professor/TA about the classes and days that you will have to miss due to athletic conflicts.
- Ask for suggestions around ways to make up missed assignments or gather missed Information.
- Follow through on make-up opportunities or offers of assistance.
- Utilize office hours.
- Know your professor's attendance policy.
- Seek assistance at the FIRST sign of difficulty or lack of understanding.

Instead of heading straight to the back of a large lecture hall, try to sit in the front. This means that you must actually be on time for class. While sitting in the front seems like a minor point, there is tremendous benefit to this action: the professor gets to see you and knows that you are engaged; there are fewer people between you and the professor, minimizing distractions and making engagement much easier to maintain; you can see and hear what is being taught much easier than if you were all the way in the back; and research indicates that students who sit in the front and middle of the class perform better on exams (Mercincavage & Brooks, 1990; Rennels & Chaudhari, 1988).

> 14% of student-athletes surveyed occasionally skipped classes their freshman year because their class sizes were large and they felt that their professors would not notice.

Another struggle for first-year students is approaching the professor or asking questions. Many student-athletes feel uncomfortable or insecure about talking to their professors; they aren't sure what to ask, they are concerned that the professor may not like them (or student-athletes in general), and are afraid of "looking silly." The result is that they choose to sit silently while actually they are struggling in the class. These feelings are common and understandable; yet not communicating with your professors

72% of upperclass student-athletes rarely or never met with their professors during office hours their freshman year.

only hurts you as a student (and as an athlete). As a student-athlete you typically have access to multiple people who can help you prepare for conversations with your professors. Your academic advisor is a good resource to utilize in helping you brainstorm strategies to approach your professors or questions to ask. Your coaches are also good places to turn for assistance in communicating with professors. They often have had a lot of experience in this area, and can take time out to help you prepare for these interactions. Ultimately, building a relationship with each of your professors is going to be vital to your success throughout the course of your academic career. Professors are not in the business of failing students, and the more interaction that you have with them the more likely it is that you will be successful in their class. Remember, if you attend every class

> "My advisor...I talked to him all the time about classes...what classes I should pick, where I can find tutors."
> *—Junior, Football*

(with the exception of competition related absences), study for tests, turn in all assignments, show interest in the course, and consistently ask for help when needed, it will be almost impossible to earn a bad grade!

Online or Hybrid Classes

Technology advances have allowed for an expansion of the traditional "classroom," as many institutions now offer online courses, or hybrid courses, which are a combination of the traditional classroom and the online classroom. Some students make the mistake of assuming that moving the teaching environment from the building across campus to the world of cyberspace will result in a less challenging class. Please don't make this mistake. Often, online courses require a great deal of time, independent effort, increased motivation to remain structured and on task, and sometimes even a different learning style. Keep in mind that professors who are responsible for building online courses have to design them in a manner that enrolled students spend an equivalent amount of time on course-related work as those physically sitting in the classroom seats across campus. Online courses require a different type of interaction, preparation, and discipline as compared to traditional courses (Merisotis & Phipps, 1999; Roval & Barnum, 2003).

There are a few things students can do to increase the possibility of success in online or hybrid classes. First, do NOT wait until the last minute to complete your assignments. It is often easy to look at the due date on your syllabus and think you have more time than you really do. Online classes are designed around continuous online discussions and you often have to be logged on for a certain time and respond within a very strict time frame. Make sure you are well aware of the allowed time frame for each of your assignments—down to the minute—which may differ for daily assignments, exams, and group work.

> "When you have discipline in your academics, you can have discipline in your sport. And when you're not stressed about your academics, you're not stressed about your sport. And it really goes hand in hand. It's really important to understand that you need to put academics first." *–Junior, Women's Volleyball*

Another important factor to consider that is related to procrastination in online classes is one of technology. Unfortunately, it is not at all uncommon for the Internet on campus to have difficulties in the last five minutes before your assignment is due. Very few professors find it easy to empathize with students who run into challenges submitting assignments—even for situations beyond their control—when it is clear they have waited until the last minute. Another suggestion for success is being knowledgeable about the academic integrity issues related to classes that have an online component, as the guidelines may be different from traditional classes regarding information sources and collaboration. Most universities that offer a large number of classes online have given professors access to software programs that scan completed assignments for plagiarism in order to monitor online academic integrity. The final note of advice is to create a separate workspace, free from distractions, and stay organized. In most ways, an online course should be treated similar to traditional courses. Use these tips to increase your likelihood of succeeding in one of these classes while being careful that you do not take shortcuts simply because a course is offered in a different format.

Reflection Time:
- *What are some of the strategies that you find to be most effective for note taking during class?*
- *What are some of the academic stereotypes of student-athletes on your campus?*
  - *How do you respond to those stereotypes?*
- *What are factors that make it difficult to ask questions in or after class?*

Mental Health Concerns in the Academic Transition

There are a number of mental health concerns that impact academic performance for all students, and there are a few common mental health issues experienced by student-athletes that are specific to the academic transition which include (but are not limited to):

learning disabilities, ADHD, depression, and anxiety. It is important that student-athletes are familiar with the signs and symptoms that may be indicative of these disorders, recognize the support available for them, and utilize those resources to increase their opportunities of success.

There is often a stigma associated with mental health related concerns that can contribute to a hesitance to seek help or navigate the proper channels when signs or symptoms occur (Eisenberg, Downs, Golberstein & Zivin, 2009; Martin, 2010; Downs & Eisenberg, 2012). At the very least, this resistance can make the academic experience more difficult than necessary, and at its worst, this resistance can set student-athletes up for academic failure. Students who are formally diagnosed can receive varying levels of accommodation—from the opportunity to have additional time, to complete exams in a distraction free environment, to the benefit of classroom note takers. If you are not aware of these services, be certain to contact either the Learning Specialist in your Athletic Academic Support Center or the director of the Office of Student Disabilities. Some first-year students express embarrassment or a sense of anxiety related to utilizing these offices on campus and choose not to use their accommodations, even when they qualify for them. Unfortunately, this will undoubtedly put them at a disadvantage academically, which in turn can negatively impact their athletic experience. Here are some common mental health related issues that can have an academic impact on student-athletes:

Learning Disorders: Learning disorders are marked by significant difficulties in learning or mastering concepts in the areas of math, reading, and/or writing (American Psychiatric Association, 2013). Some student-athletes enter college having already been diagnosed with a learning disorder, while others may not begin to recognize their disability until college, as a result of the increased academic demands. In other words, if you find yourself struggling significantly in one of these three areas (reading, writing, or math) it may be helpful to explore the possibility of completing a formal learning assessment. Universities will either provide the testing internally or have access to community resources that can provide such an assessment. Formal testing and diagnosis can lead to the creation of a learning plan and effective treatment that will allow a student-athlete to be more successful in their efforts to learn and retain information—both in the classroom as well as on the athletic field.

Attention Deficit Hyperactivity Disorder (ADHD): Similar to learning disorders, some students enter college with a previous diagnosis of ADHD, a disorder that is marked by impulsivity, difficulty in focus and concentration, easy distractibility, and inattention (American Psychiatric Association, 2013). On the other hand, there are also many students who do not recognize these symptoms until they enter college. Though this disorder can be over diagnosed, there are many students who meet the criteria for this disorder and struggle academically as a result. Student-athletes who are experiencing this disorder, or who possess these symptoms should understand their options and explore potential support systems. If you are concerned about possible symptoms of ADHD, we recommend you begin by seeking assistance from your campus Academic Support Center or Disabilities Services Office as well as your Athletic Academic Support staff.

Depression: It is not uncommon for the first year of college to be one of several adjustments, which can be extremely stressful. Consider the multiple academic stressors of college: tests, papers, exams, and overall greater demands. When stress is not managed well, symptoms of depression may occur. Unfortunately, many students are unclear about the line between "normal" stress, feelings of sadness, being overwhelmed, and signs that may be indicators of something more significant. Symptoms of depression include difficulty with concentration and focus, increased isolation, irritability, fatigue, and sadness. With these symptoms, it is easy to see how a student would have difficulty remaining focused in classes or while studying. In extreme cases, students struggle to find the motivation to get out of bed to attend class or the attention and focus to sit down and study when they need to. When an individual's early depressive symptoms continue to be ignored, they can build into a sense of hopelessness and helplessness, and in some cases eventually lead to thoughts of self-harm or suicide. Therefore, it is extremely important that you are able to recognize these early signs, understand their impact, and utilize the resources available to help manage them.

Anxiety: Finally, anxiety is one of the most common mental health related concerns, and is characterized by worry about the past or apprehension about the future (American Psychiatric Association, 2013). Everyone experiences anxiety in some situations, and in small amounts, it can actually be helpful. For example, without a healthy and relatively small amount of anxiety about failing a test, you may not feel motivated to study. Similarly, a moderate amount of anxiety about an upcoming game can be helpful in ensuring you practice and prepare with enough effort. Conversely, you may experience anxiety in some situations when you know that you have not prepared enough and are afraid of failing (or being embarrassed) as a result.

For many first-year student-athletes, anxiety may be the result of the increased pressure to perform at a higher level. This may be the first time that you have been challenged academically, or you may be concerned about the impact of your grades on athletic eligibility. When this worry or concern becomes too frequent or is triggered too easily, it can become debilitating and actually impede performance, both academically and athletically. In the academic realm, too much anxiety can contribute to 'freezing' when you enter a situation where you may be evaluated, such as an exam or presentation. This can happen despite a high level of preparation and readiness. If you are finding yourself worrying a great deal or you are struggling to perform despite the work and effort you have put into preparing, it may be helpful to seek support to help you manage the anxiety.

Concussion Management: We end this section with a discussion about concussions, as they are becoming more prevalent and more frequently diagnosed (Center for Disease Control, 2013). This increase of diagnosis is leading university athletic departments to create or strengthen their concussion protocol. As there is evidence that head injuries can have a significant impact on learning and in some cases, present emotional and behavioral symptoms such as sadness, irritability, or impulsivity, it is important to recognize the larger implications of sustaining head injuries (Van Noordt & Good, 2011; Halstead, et. al, 2013; Hylin, et. al, 2013). Results of head injuries go beyond behavioral symptoms and impact classroom performance in the form of short-term memory loss, difficulty concentrating, and vision impairment. Many athletic training departments inform faculty when student-athletes sustain a concussion, requesting some consideration of the possible symptoms that may impact learning during that time. In rare cases, an untreated concussion—combined with continuous play—can magnify the effect of symptoms and increase the likelihood of subsequent concussions. Again, it is important that you communicate with your coaches and training staff when a head injury is sustained. The long-term consequences can sometimes far outweigh the short-term pressure you may feel to return to competition before your body is ready.

Medication Management

An additional factor to consider under the larger mental health umbrella is medication management. A formal diagnosis of some mental health issues includes a recommendation for medication; again, if this is your situation, be willing to follow through and gain the benefit that this form of treatment will provide. When medication is a part of your treatment protocol, it is also important that you follow it consistently and accurately.

This means making sure you take your medication at roughly the same time daily, making certain not to consume foods or other substances that interact with your medication, and ensuring that you do not misuse it. Since student-athletes are required to undergo random testing for substances, be sure to communicate with your athletic training staff about your medications so they are able to submit appropriate documentation to the NCAA.

Reflection Time:
- *How have you sought help for academic difficulties?*
- *What would be a barrier that would prevent you from using the resources in this area?*

International Students and the Academic Transition

International student-athletes may experience unique challenges related to their academic transition. Dependent upon your home country, some of you will face language barriers, be accustomed to different teaching styles, or feel intimidated and overwhelmed by the overall learning environment. In some cases, having English as a second language can impact all aspects of the first-year academic experience. Classroom learning may be impacted, as some students may struggle to keep up with the speech patterns and speaking rate of the professor. You may struggle to understand the use of terms, comprehend the lecture, and simultaneously take notes. This language barrier can also impact utilization of academic resources, as it may contribute to difficulties working with tutors or participating in study and work groups.

If there is a language barrier, it is important that you speak with your professor as early in the semester as possible to address this issue. This may lead to individual meetings with the instructor to review information before or after class. Additionally, it helps your professor make efforts to teach you better. For example, they may work to speak more slowly in class or limit their use of jargon and local vernacular. However, you will have to communicate your language deficiencies in order for the professor to help you succeed.

If English is your second language, you should realistically assess the time you will need to complete assignments. The language barrier often means that completing assignments, reading, writing, and test taking will require longer time than it would in your native language. Make sure you take this time into consideration when you are building your schedule, selecting your courses, preparing to study or complete assignments, and even choosing your major. You will want to make full use of the Writing Center and the resources available there, as this can significantly decrease the time you may have to spend to complete assignments on your own and teach you skills that can be used on future assignments. Finally, build a relationship with the international student associations and the international student office to make connections and find support. They may also have additional resources or be able to provide guidance to help you navigate your academic transition. For example, they may know about academic courses designed to allow English as a second language students (ESL) practice speaking and develop their language skills.

Transfer Students and the Academic Transition

In many ways the academic transition for transfer students parallels the transition experienced by first-year student-athletes. To a certain degree, this adjustment may even be easier for you since you have already had the first-year academic experience at your previous institution. You have learned to balance the unstructured schedule, read and follow the syllabus, and understand the amount of effort needed to compete academically. While this prior experience is helpful, there are still a number of factors that could positively or negatively impact your academic transition as a transfer student-athlete. Here are few things that you should consider as you are managing this adjustment.

3 Things Transfers Should Do to Adjust Academically

- **Know your academic record and double check it as soon as you arrive on campus.** In some situations, transfer students learn too late that the courses or credits that they thought would transfer did not. As soon as you get to your new institution, take the initiative to follow up with your academic advisor—and the registrar's office—to secure your academic standing, your credit hours earned, academic eligibility based on GPA, and progress toward degree attainment. It is your responsibility to be clear on this point, as you are the one ultimately impacted by any discrepancies that leave you academically ineligible or further away from degree completion.

  > 57% of upperclass student-athletes rarely or never spoke with their academic advisors about academic eligibility requirements during their first year.

- **Choose a major based on both academic and athletic factors.** Transfer student-athletes need to choose a major that allows enough credit hours to transfer in and remain academically eligible to compete athletically. Similarly, while it is tempting to choose a major strictly for athletic purposes, it is also important to focus on long term career aspirations and job potential. As a transfer student, it is very important to work with your academic advisor to ensure that your choice in major maximizes the remainder of your college career for long-term gain.

- **Use your resources, even if you don't think you need them**. Many transfer students had the experience of mandatory study halls and required use of tutors at their first institution. As a result, they may feel it is unnecessary to make use of these resources at their new school. Getting off to a good start at your new institution is imperative to your progress toward degree completion, continued academic eligibility, and retention. For example, transfer students tend to fail their first round of exams. Use the resources available to you to prevent you from falling into that pattern. You should not view the use of tutors, the writing center, and study hall as punitive or unnecessary, but rather consider them important to your overall academic success.

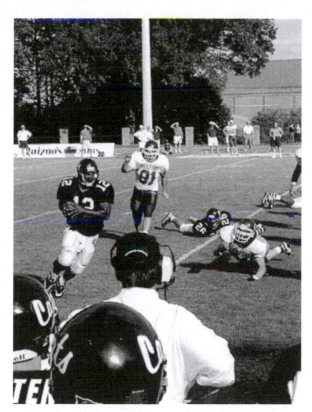

Discussion Questions

1. What are the biggest differences between your high school and college classes?

2. How many hours or credits are required for graduation in your anticipated major?

3. What are the NCAA's academic requirements for student-athletes to remain academically eligible to compete at your institution?

4. What are three specific things that you can do this week that will improve your current position in your most challenging class?

Journal Space

_____

_____

_____

_____

_____

_____

_____

_____

Chapter 2: The Athletic Transition

All first-year college students, both athletes and non-athletes, have to manage the social and academic transition from high school to college. As we highlight throughout this text, your athletic role can impact your ability to juggle the new social and academic opportunities. However, many first-year student-athletes find the most difficult transition that they experience is on the playing fields or courts. High school, travel, club, and Amateur Athletic Union (AAU) sports have evolved dramatically over the last 20 years, and first-year student-athletes are now coming to college with a great deal of experience in highly competitive environments. Today's first-year college athletes also come to campuses with a high level of physical training and sport specific instruction. In short, freshmen student-athletes arrive on college campuses bigger, stronger, faster and more experienced.

Despite the higher level of playing experience and physical training that athletes have upon entering college, the athletic learning curve that you face when transitioning from high school to college sports is very steep and in most cases, unavoidable. If you are currently feeling out of place and questioning your athletic abilities, understand that your thoughts are normal and felt by thousands of other first-year athletes across the country. Most first-year student-athletes find the athletic transition to be a challenging one, in spite of previous training or athletic ability.

Level of Competition

While it is true that today's freshman student-athletes come to campus with a great deal of playing experience, very few understand the day-to-day physical and mental demands that are required to earn consistent playing time at the collegiate level. The vast majority of college athletes were the most physically gifted and athletically talented players on their high school and club teams, but unfortunately talent alone is not enough to earn first-year student-athletes the playing time that they may want or expect.

> "To a freshman student-athlete… I'd say that they'd better be prepared to work, and be prepared to work harder than they ever thought they could. College sports are a whole different level from high school."
> -Senior, Men's Track and Field

Once you arrive on campus, you begin to compete for playing time in a much different way than you ever have in your career. Prior to your first year in college, you may have earned or maintained your playing time based on how you performed during athletic events. As first-year collegiate athletes, most of your previous successes and failures are minimized, and coaches solely evaluate performance based on how you compete and perform daily in training and competition. This can be a difficult adjustment for many because they are accustomed to getting opportunities to showcase their talents during competition regardless of how they have performed in practice or in the weight room. However, the majority of college coaches want to see their players perform consistently in training before they trust them enough to allow them to compete; this can be an especially tough transition to navigate.

Unfortunately, many first-year athletes have never been required to prove themselves on a daily basis to earn playing time. This new level of physical and mental expectation and exertion can be overwhelming for some athletes. As a result, some first-year athletes have a difficult time performing consistently either in practice or games because they fail to positively respond to these daily demands and pressures. The best way to manage this is by treating practice and training (or the weight room) like an actual game or event, bringing the same amount of physical and mental energy. Coaches determine playing time based on your performance during practice; as a result, you must first win on the practice fields and in the weight room before you are given the opportunity to win during competition. Here are some ways to ensure a high level of effort in practice.

---

7 Ways to Perform in Practice

- Create practice goals.
- Approach practice with a plan.
- View practice as an opportunity to prepare for competition, rather than something to "get through."
- Know your playbook or competition plan.
- Share your goals with teammates or coaches.
- Identify one or two areas where you can improve technically, and work on that before and after practice or training.
- Meet with your coaches periodically to seek feedback and get a better understanding of how you are performing and what you need to do to improve.

Navigating Playing Time

While there are always exceptions to the rule, most first-year athletes struggle to earn significant playing time. This is simply a hard fact of being a first-year student-athlete! Unfortunately, earning playing time at the collegiate level is impacted by a multitude of factors, much more than simply being physically gifted in your sport. For example, some first-year athletes struggle earning playing time because they are learning new systems, training methods, teammates, and coaching styles. This learning curve can impact your ability to perform consistently. As a freshman, everything is new and it may feel as though things are moving rapidly on campus. As you try to process this new information, you are often forced to do a great deal of thinking. However, there are some performance situations where too much thinking can hinder the ability to execute. Think about it....when you are performing at your best—when you are in the "zone"—you are not thinking at all. Your brain is shut off and your body is automatically working at an optimal level. It is extremely difficult to compete at your best when your brain is overloaded with information.

Another contributing factor is the competition against older and more physically mature athletes who have more experience training and playing at the collegiate level. As a first-year athlete you will be competing against (in practice and competition) athletes who are already accustomed to the level of competition, more sophisticated systems/playbooks and coaching styles at their respective colleges. Equally (or more importantly,) veteran college athletes have a better understanding of what it takes mentally and physically to be successful at this level. So again, if you find yourself not playing as much as you would like, don't get discouraged. The transition from high school to college is a difficult one, and you must work extremely hard to break into the starting lineup of any sport...especially in your first year!

> 52% of upperclass student-athletes reported having felt at times that they were not as talented as their teammates during their first year.

Without a doubt, upperclassmen walk into most situations with an advantage. They know the coaches and understand the coaching philosophies and systems. Upperclass student athletes have a level of comfort that first-year athletes do not get for many weeks after being on campus because they know seemingly silly things like where the cafeteria is and how to line up for stretching prior to practice. This knowledge and comfort level gives upperclassmen an advantage because they can focus on their performance and do not have to spend time learning and worrying about the basics. Please understand that this in no way means that upperclassmen are more talented than freshmen.

There is a significant learning curve for first-year athletes and you will have to work especially hard to overcome the experience advantage that upperclassmen possess. To minimize the impact on your playing time, be intentional about learning your coach's expectations, philosophy and strategy as soon as you can. The good news for you is that you have the ability to decrease this learning curve and put yourself in position to earn more playing time by going above and beyond. Study your playbook, stay late or come early to practice, and spend more time with your coaches.

It is true that most first-year athletes will have to scratch and claw to earn playing time. However, it is important that you do not let this be disheartening. Too often there is a pattern that emerges when first-year players do not do a good job of managing the lack of playing time. Frustration and disappointment can build up, causing some athletes to respond by giving less than their best effort in practice and competition. At times, you may feel that no matter how well you perform, you will not get the playing time you think you deserve. This disillusionment can lead to lack of engagement and cause you to place less importance on training, which will ultimately have a negative impact on your performance. This pattern can create a self-fulfilling prophecy where you may be performing below standard and your coaches are not able to use you in competition because you are not prepared mentally or physically to compete. Do not let this happen to you!

Reflection Time:
- *What are three steps you can take to increase your potential for gaining greater playing time?*
- *What are some negative responses to a lack of playing time that you have witnessed from current or former teammates?*

Navigating the Red-Shirt Transition

Most of the information you will receive about your first-year of college athletics will refer to athletes who are currently on active rosters, and you will receive limited information about the different experiences encountered by those who have decided (voluntarily or involuntarily) to red-shirt their first-year may encounter. Red-shirting can be viewed in a number of different ways. Some athletes look at red-shirting as a negative, and think this means that they are not as talented as their peers. Others may believe that red-shirting suggests that they will never have the opportunity to compete at this level. We believe that making this choice can (and should) be viewed positively.

The decision to red-shirt allows athletes an opportunity to acclimate themselves to their sport, and the classroom, without the pressures of

> "**Training knowing that you're not going to be competing is really rough. There were times when I didn't want to come to practice. I didn't want to go get treatment. I didn't want to do anything...I just wanted to go home... relax...go out...you know...have fun...because there is no competition. I really didn't have anything to worry about. But at the same time it's more the long term that you have to really look at. If I don't fix this injury now, next year when I do want to come back I'm going to get injured again.**" *-Junior, Women's Track & Field*

competing right away. Athletes that red-shirt their first year can potentially benefit academically from this decision. They are able to focus more on academics because they do not have the same athletic responsibilities as their teammates who do not red-shirt. In fact, many athletes who sit out a year are able to graduate early or take lighter academic loads as a 5th year senior, some are even able to work on a master's degree while completing their athletic eligibility. In addition to the academic benefits, there can also be athletic benefits to red-shirting. Athletes who do not compete during their first year are typically stronger and faster than their competition during their final year of eligibility. Similarly, these athletes have the advantage of being more mentally mature than the athletes they are competing against.

While there are many potential benefits to red-shirting, there are a number of challenges that can arise if athletes do not view it as an opportunity. One possible drawback is the isolation or loneliness that athletes might feel as a result of being unable to participate in competition, particularly if the rest of your first-year class is actively gaining competition experience. It can also be a challenge to remain motivated and connected to your teammates and coaches when you are not competing for playing time. Furthermore, there may be additional stressors to navigate based on the circumstances surrounding the decision to red-shirt, for example managing an injury or increasing your GPA. It may feel as though your coaches and teammates do not value you in the same way as they do athletes on the active roster, and while many times this is our perception and not reality, some athletes can become unmotivated or upset by their situations.

While it may be difficult to see in the moment, red-shirting should be a positive experience for athletes. If this becomes the best option for you, just remember, you are not alone. Student-athletes have been making the decision to red-shirt for decades; the first noted student-athlete did so in 1939, and this decision resulted in two All-American years ("Warren Alfson", 2013). So keep in mind that having to sit out your first year does not have to be without benefit. There are several ways to use that time as an opportunity to prepare for success during your four years of eligibility.

<u>10 Ways to Make the Most of Your Red-Shirt Year</u>

- **Take advantage of the time to get ahead academically**. For example, if it is appropriate for you, take the maximum number of credit hours that you can. Spend time becoming more familiar with the academic support and additional resources that your university offers.

- **Get involved in other on-campus activities that may not necessarily be sports related**. This involvement can serve you well, as you will develop relationships with students across campus and majors.

- **Devote time and energy to getting bigger, faster, and stronger**. Take advantage of the practice time to get better at your sport and improve your game.

- **Use the time to become more familiar with your team's playbook or more knowledgeable about team approach and strategy**. Be proactive and develop the skills to be a leader on your team.

- **Spend some time in your university's career center and become familiar with the services they offer**. Use the time to develop interview skills, learn to write a resume, or take a business etiquette class.

- **Try to find an internship or work-study position that will allow you to develop some hands-on work experience.** Utilize your time wisely, and plan for your future.

- **Engage in community service or volunteer activities.** These are experiences that could potentially turn into an internship at some point.

- **Spend some energy making sure that you keep your support systems intact**. This can also be an opportunity for those who have limited support systems to begin to develop one.

- **If an injury is a contributing cause to your decision to red-shirt, spend the time and energy to focus on rehabbing**. It can be difficult to remain motivated when you know you won't compete, but this is the chance to increase the likelihood of success when you return, and decrease the possibility of re-injury.

- **Use the time to further develop relationships with your coaches, athletic trainers, and teammates**. It might be easy to disconnect from your team when you are not competing, so be intentional about building and maintaining those relationships.

Reflection Time:

- *If you have decided to red-shirt, what are three ways you can take advantage of your decision?*

Navigating New Relationships

The Coach-Athlete Relationship

First-year student-athletes must quickly adjust to the business of college athletics. On the one hand, the essence of the games athletes play at a collegiate level are similar to the sports they have been playing all of their lives. On the other hand, college athletics is an entirely different undertaking. One major difference that first-year students recognize right away is the singular focus of their

> **10% of upperclass student-athletes frequently felt isolated from their coaches during their first year.**

coaches. College coaches eat, sleep, and breathe their sport. This may be different from the coaches that most athletes have had in the past. Many high school coaches coach multiple sports, teach classes, or have outside jobs that require some of their attention. At the collegiate level, most coaches are employed specifically to coach, so they spend every hour of the day strategizing about the next opponent and/or recruiting their next star athlete. As a result, college coaches often don't have as much time to devote to cultivating player/coach relationships.

The demanding schedule of a college coach often results in limited relationships with first-year athletes. The relationships that do form are focused primarily on sports related issues. This may occur for a number of reasons. For college coaches, success is often defined by winning games and they may appear to be obsessive about athletic performance and outcomes. Secondly, college coaches do not have the prolonged history with their players that many of the club and high school coaches have, and therefore athletes may not feel the same deep connection they are accustomed to.

> "I think coming to school and fitting in with the coach was one of the biggest challenges. When I was recruited I kind of expected more when I got here, but that's when I realized that things were a bit different. And I had to deal with that for myself and I'm pretty sure that affected me athletically."-*Junior, Men's Golf*

Often, high school and club coaches are people who have been fixtures in a community, and may have worked with some athletes since childhood. This typically means that club and high school coaches know a great deal about their athletes both on and off the field and are able to connect with their players in a different way than most college coaches. It is important to remember that you were recruited to be a member of your college team primarily because of your ability to help that team be successful. As a result, your expectation of the relationship with your coach may need to be adjusted. This does not mean that college coaches will not and cannot have great relationships with their players; it just means that both the players and coaches have to work hard to build this relationship. An athlete's relationship with their coach is important at every level of competition, but it's imperative that first-year athletes learn how to navigate the relationship early on for a successful transition.

Another way that the business end of college athletics reveals itself is the change that may occur in your relationship with your coach after the recruiting process is complete, once you arrive on campus. Many first-year student-athletes choose their college based on their connection with the coaching staff; however, that relationship may shift when you arrive on campus and pre-season begins. Once you become a college athlete, the role of your coach shifts from recruiter to teacher. Athletes should be conscious of the possibility of this changing role and relationship, and prepare themselves accordingly. It is important to realize that great coaches are constantly looking at the future; once an athlete commits to their program, coaches begin to focus on team rather than individual athlete success. Many first-year student-athletes are surprised at how different their coaches are once they arrive on campus; preparing yourself for this potential change can help to reduce a potentially negative reaction.

With effort and opportunity, you should be able to cultivate a healthy relationship with at least one member of your coaching staff. However, it is probably unrealistic to expect the same type of relationship with your head coach that you had with your high school or club coaches. At the collegiate level it is common—and necessary—for athletes to develop meaningful relationships with their assistant coaches as well. In addition to providing support and guidance, assistant coaches can provide athletic based feedback, valuable perspective on the game and help you maximize your overall college experience.

---

5 Great Ways to Develop a Relationship With Your College Coach

- **Meet regularly, in a one on one format**. Depending on your schedule and theirs, frequent interaction will allow you to get a better sense of your coach's preferences and expectations as well as your areas of improvement.

- **Talk to your coach about who you are outside of your sport**. This allows your coach to get to know you as a whole person, which can help them coach you better.

- **Act on the feedback that your coaches give you**. Coaches like to see that their athletes are listening and can apply the feedback that they give. And if you ask your coach for feedback...put it to use!

- **Don't participate in negative conversations or gossip regarding your coaching staff**. Athletic teams are small communities. This is not a healthy or effective way to build a relationship.

- **Be honest with your coaches, and if something bad happens, be the first person to tell them**. Do not allow someone else to tell your story. Coaches appreciate honesty and often don't like surprises. They are typically more willing and able to help if they feel that they have the entire story before things get out of hand.

Coaching Styles

One factor that may be helpful in navigating the relationship with your coach is gaining a general understanding of your coach's individual coaching style. Developing an understanding of each style can help you cultivate skills that will allow you to perform in a way that matches your coach's style and get the most out of your coaching relationship. Research indicates there are three widely accepted coaching styles—autocratic, democratic, and accommodating— and in order for you to be most effective in interacting with your coach it will be helpful for you to know common characteristics of each type (Chelladurai & Saleh, 1978). Understanding each coaching style will enable you to adapt your communication and interactions to optimize your relationship with your coach.

> "You have to listen to your coaching staff, because they'll tell you that you're working too hard. Your body isn't going to be able to sustain it....especially with track. In college we have longer, more intense work-outs. And that puts a lot of strain on the body. Some-times we'll have a hard work out, and the next day we'll have another hard workout. A lot of people think their bodies are adjusted to it, but it's not. So listen to your coaching staff...go to see your trainer instead of think-ing, oh, I can run through it, I can practice through it. You've got to handle that in the beginning."
> *-Sophomore, Women's Track & Field*

Autocratic: Typically coaches who display an autocratic coaching style assume all respon-sibility for team decisions in a directive and decisive manner. They rarely seek feedback or input from athletes when managing team situations, and at times may appear inflexible and critical. These coaches often seem to motivate by fear, and athletes may find it difficult to feel connected or appreciated.

Democratic: Coaches who exhibit a democratic coaching style tend to integrate student-athlete feedback into their coaching decisions. While coaches with a democratic style maintain ultimate decision-making power, they also recognize the value of their athletes and assistant's opinions and suggestions. Democratic coaches understand the benefits of sharing responsibility for team success and create an environment where each in-dividual feels empowered to contribute.

> "But it is very important to stay open with your coach. Even when they don't want to know about your personal life, if something's going on, you need to share it with them. So, the more open you are with your coach, the better relationship you're going to have. Especially with things like injuries. Never act like you aren't injured because it could build into something worse. And most coaches are going to be upset or annoyed that you didn't tell them. So, communication is a big, big thing."
> *-Junior, Women's Track & Field*

Accommodating: Coaches with an accommodating style typically do not make decisions quickly or decisively, and they may defer responsibility to their assistant coaches or student-athletes. Coaches who fit this style may be burned out or struggle to enjoy their coaching duties. Student-athletes may find it difficult to trust these coaches due to their lack of consistency or structure.

Below are a few descriptive terms for each coaching style.

Autocratic	Democratic	Accommodating
Rigid	Flexible	Inconsistent
Forceful	Patient	Indecisive
Aggressive	Assertive	Passive
Formal	Relational	Overly emotional
Ego-Driven	Confident	Insecure

In addition to understanding each coaching style, it is also important to recognize the expectations that each style has of their athletes. Here are some common characteristics that each coaching style tends to value.

Coaching Style Expectations

Autocratic	Democratic	Accommodating
Structure	Verbal and emotional expression	Self-directed
Limited questions	Inquisitive	Decisive
Business-like approach	Relational	Agreeable
Emotional control	Provide feedback	Low maintenance and self-sufficient
Quick implementation of feedback	Cooperation	

Reflection Time:
- *What is your coach's coaching style? Please provide evidence.*
- *Which style would you use to describe your favorite coach?*
- *What are three steps you can take to work better with your current coach and their style?*

Teammate Relationships

The transition into college athletics also proves to be difficult for some first-year athletes because the concept of team and teammate really changes at this level. Many first-year athletes are surprised at the barriers that they perceive between themselves and their teammates once they arrive on campus. College sports definitely revolve around the team concept, but at the collegiate level both players and coaches are striving to reach greater individual heights and achievements. Some coaches are attempting to coach their way into higher profile coaching positions, and many college athletes are hoping to use college sports as a springboard into professional or elite sports. These realizations change the landscape of what *team* means in intercollegiate athletics. First-year athletes have to embrace the idea that everyone on their team wants to play (including themselves), and no one is happy sitting on the bench or not contributing to the team. Thus, many first-year athletes may be viewed as a threat to playing time by their teammates.

Most collegiate athletes are coming from high school experiences where their teammates were their best friends. As a result, they may be unprepared for this shift in dynamics, and it can sometimes contribute to additional pressure and unnecessary conflict. As a first-year athlete, you must recognize and understand the resistance that you may feel from your teammates. In many ways, from the time you walk on campus you are competing both with and against each other. You must be prepared to work hard to earn the respect of your teammates, appreciating that there is a significant part of college athletics that is all about competition.

If it's helpful, try to remember your experience as a high school senior, and how you viewed underclassmen that were working to prove themselves. Your current teammates want you on the team because they know that the team is better with you, but you must also understand that everyone is vying for playing time and your teammates may not be so eager to have a newcomer challenge them. Many college teams have more than one first-year athlete entering at the same time, and depending on the situation, it can be sometimes easier to develop a relationship with other first-year student-athletes than with upper class teammates.

---

5 Ways to Develop Positive Relationships with Your Teammates:

- **Partner with an upperclassman and ask for guidance.**
- **Attend every optional and mandatory pre-season activity.**
- **Accept offers by your teammates to hang out and bond.**
- **Use academics as a way to connect with your teammates.** Find out who has taken your classes and/or professors before, and ask them what you can expect.
- **If you have teammates or other athletes in your classes, offer to share notes or ask them if they are interested in forming a study group.** A study group would be helpful for you academically, but a study group would also give you an opportunity to get to know your teammates in a different context.

Your ability to successfully navigate these new teammate relationships will be dependent on a variety of factors, including the size of the team, the nature of the sport, and the distribution of upperclassmen. One way that teams can help first-years develop good relationships is by pairing them with upperclassmen mentors. During pre-season (or prior to arriving on campus) ask your coach or team captain if such a program already exists. Another way to develop healthy teammate relationships is by attending pre-season camps, which often include team-building and bonding exercises. Be aware of characteristics of others that you tend to find supportive, and work to actively seek out relationships with members of your team who may fit that criteria. One of the ways the NCAA helps teams build healthy relationships and strengthen team dynamics is by having student-athletes complete the DiSC® assessment. The DiSC® is an assessment tool designed to improve productivity, teamwork and communication within groups. DiSC® profiles can provide information about how you and your team are motivated, resolve conflict and solve problems. Used within the context of sports teams, it can help individuals and teams communicate more effectively and understand each other's needs. This assessment outlines four behavior patterns (Dominance, Influence, Steadiness and Conscientiousness), which can then be explored in an effort to enhance relationships, increase productivity, and build team cohesion. Each style is briefly outlined below (Disc® Classic Validation, 2008).

> 13% of upperclass student-athletes reported feeling frequently isolated from their teammates during their first year.

Dominance: People with this primary style place an emphasis on achieving results; they are motivated by winning and success. Individuals with this predominant style readily accept challenges and push for immediate results. As a result, they are complemented by others who use caution, research facts, and weigh pros and cons prior to making decisions. When communicating with someone with this predominant style, you benefit from providing them with key details, focusing on identifying a solution versus highlighting the problems, and being very brief and specific.

Influence: People with this primary style place an emphasis on influencing and persuading others. A person with this style enjoys group activities, building relationships, and collaborating with others. These individuals enjoy being coached and having the freedom to express themselves. People with an Influencing predominate style are complemented by individuals who speak directly, seek facts, and develop systematic approaches. When you are communicating with someone with a predominate "I" style, you should share your experiences, allow time for questions, focus on the positives, avoid giving too much detail, and try not to interrupt them.

Steadiness: People with this primary style place an emphasis on cooperating with others to carry out the task. A person with an "S" style is motivated by cooperation, helping others and being appreciated. These individuals are characterized as calm, predictable and deliberate. They tend to be consistent and resistant to change. People with this style are complemented by individuals who respond well to change, can manage multiple tasks at once and can set priorities effectively. When communicating with someone whose primary style is an "S," you benefit from clearly expressing your expectations and avoiding overly aggressive or confrontational behaviors.

Conscientiousness: People with this primary style place an emphasis on working carefully to ensure quality and accuracy. A person with a "C" style is motivated by an opportunity to learn new things and the desire to complete projects accurately. They may be described as cautious, systematic, and precise. They can benefit from working with others who can make quick decisions, aren't afraid to state unpopular positions, and who encourage teamwork. When communicating with someone with this predominant style, you may benefit from a diplomatic approach, focusing on facts or details rather than emotion.

There are a few important factors to remember when reviewing the DiSC® behavioral styles. There is not a preferred style or style that leads to greater success academically or athletically. Additionally, most of us fluctuate between styles depending on the environment and the situation. We encourage you to use the style information provided to both gain self-awareness, and to develop ways to effectively communicate and interact with your coaches and teammates.

Reflection Time:
- *What do you think is your style?*
- *What would be the style of your teammates you find to be most supportive?*
- *What is the style that is the most challenging for you to interact or work with?*

DiSC® Styles

Dominance	Influence
Results Oriented	Articulate
Enjoys Challenges	Likes to Persuade
Makes Quick Decisions	Enthusiastic
Problem Solver	Entertaining
Enjoys leading	Motivator
Conscientiousness	**Steadiness**
Detail Oriented	Consistent
Analytical	Predictable
Accurate	Patient
Systematic	Loyal
Value quality	Calm

Some coaches will use this assessment as a way for their teams to learn about each other and find a way to work together more effectively. If this is not something your team currently does, find out if it is something you may be able to do as a team.

Reflection Time:
- *How would you describe those high school teammates who you felt were the most supportive? Challenging?*
- *Based on the chart, how would you communicate most effectively with each style?*

Injury

Most first-year student-athletes come to college physically healthy, having limited experience with major injuries. Due to the intensity and duration of training at the collegiate level, navigating injuries becomes a necessity. Obviously, injuries don't occur to every athlete and hopefully you will be lucky enough to avoid that experience. Yet, the reality is that many athletes face the challenge of competing through injury at some point in their careers, and first-year athletes may be particularly prone to injury due to multiple environmental changes. As the level of practice and play is higher at the collegiate level than it was in high school, there is a greater risk of injury. While we acknowledge that the risk of injury increases, there are preventative measures that you can take to minimize that risk.

> "Dealing with injuries and pressure definitely was one of my biggest challenges I think. Coming from high school I really didn't do anything. I'd just lay around at practice and then do a little bit and I managed to get by. But then coming here, I kind of thought, I wasn't improving fast enough. I pushed myself too hard and got hurt." *-Sophomore, Men's Cross Country*

8 Ways to Help Prevent Injury

- Self-care – Eat well, get enough sleep, hydrate.
- Wear the proper gear.
- Stretch, stretch, stretch.
- Cool down.
- Recognize the difference between "good" pain and "bad" pain.
- If you feel something abnormal, get it checked out.
- Use every resource available to you (team or campus doctors, etc.).
- Manage stress both on and off the field.

While we mention that injury is a common occurrence, it is also important to realize that injury doesn't just have a physical impact— it can also take a psychological toll. When athletes become injured, they run the risk of losing confidence and feeling disconnected and isolated, and they may even begin to struggle academically (Ardern, Taylor, Feller & Webster, 2013). As a result, first-year student-athletes who become injured are at a significant disadvantage. Not only are they trying to navigate their position on the team, their injury might prevent them from being a fully contributing member. This can result in fewer opportunities to socialize with teammates and spend time with coaches. It may also be difficult to remain motivated to attend practice or work through the rehab process. Injured athletes typically don't receive positive reinforcement for their actions in the same way that they do when they are healthy and participating fully. This lack of support may discourage injured athletes, thus prolonging their rehabilitation time. Navigating an injury as a first-year student-athlete can be complex, requiring the utilization of a cohesive support system (trainers, teammates, coaches, therapist, advisor, family). Here are some signs that your injury may be having more than just a physical impact.

10 Psychological Impacts of Sports Injuries

- Excessive worrying about re-injury
- Depression
- Anger
- Feelings of helplessness
- Decreases in confidence
- Poor academic performance
- Feeling isolated from teammates and coaches
- Loss of identity
- Alcohol/drug use
- Changes in sleep and appetite

- *Describe the most significant injury you have had to date.*
- *Where there any contributing factors to your injury?*
- *What could you have done differently?*
- *Identify three actions you can take to help you manage an injury.*

Self-Care

Never before has self-care played such an important role in multiple aspects of your life (Burke, Keins & Ivy, 2004; Laquale, 2007; Venter, 2012; Bird, 2013). Though it likely sounds relatively simplistic, 'the basics' are vital to performance, and at the collegiate level they can be surprisingly difficult to manage. "Self-care" is exactly what the term suggests: your ability and need to take care of yourself. Activities such as eating a balanced diet, remaining hydrated, and getting enough sleep contribute to both athletic and academic success. However, one of the thoughts expressed by so many upperclass student-athletes is surprise over how quickly their concept of time changed once they began school. When your days are filled with activities and you are attempting to balance multiple demands, time seems to move awful quickly, and you can find yourself struggling to fit in those necessities of life.

It is not uncommon for student-athletes to struggle during that first year with finding the right time to eat their meals- not too early to still be hungry during practice time, but not too late to feel like it weighs you down. Additionally, morning workouts require that you wake up early enough to be able to consume at least a small amount of food to provide the energy necessary to perform. This need has sort of a "domino effect," as now you have to factor in an earlier bedtime to allow yourself to get the amount of sleep you need to both wake up early and to perform well. Add in the fact that the nature of a college schedule is flexible and variable, meaning that everyday your class times may be different. This variability requires yet another possible change to accommodate.

Nutrition

As mentioned earlier, proper nutrition is important for optimal sport performance, and it can be extremely challenging to maintain a healthy diet in college, especially for first-year athletes. Some of the biggest challenges that athletes have around nutrition include the variety of times food is available, the enormity of high calorie, fast food options available, the lack of knowledge about how nutrition and food choices contribute to peak performance, and

> **20% of upperclass student-athletes reported that they rarely or never ate a well-balanced meal during their first year.**

learning how to eat well on the road. Another challenge that sometimes occurs is proper weight maintenance with first-year student-athletes who participate in "weight restricted" or "appearance heavy" sports, such as wrestling, swimming and diving, gymnastics, and cross-country/track and field. Due to lack of knowledge about healthy food choices and how they impact performance, you may struggle with maintaining appropriate weight, overeating, and/or poor nutrient/vitamin balance.

---

5 Nutritional Challenges of Many First-year College Students

- Finding the "right" time during the day to consume major meals.
- Consuming the proper balance of carbohydrates, fats, proteins, and sugars.
- Planning ahead in order to avoid skipping meals.
- Consuming the proper number of calories to optimize performance.
- Making appropriate post-competition meal decisions.

Most college students are surrounded by food. Many campus events offer food as an incentive to increase student attendance; most cafeterias and dining halls allow students to eat as much as they want, and return multiple times. As a result, all students—not just student-athletes—are faced with the need to establish healthy habits around food. The difference between student-athletes and the general student population is the cost that student-athletes pay for poor food choices and unhealthy diets. Research suggests that most students are unaware of what their body requires to function optimally (Burns, Schiller, Merrick & Wolf, 2004). While you may have been forced to learn the food pyramid in middle school health class, there have been a number of adaptations since that time. Additionally, depending on your sport, the number of calories you need to consume daily to maintain adequate weight and engage in proper training may significantly differ from the 2,000 calorie/day diet that most adults are suggested to maintain. For example, swimmers may burn upwards of 2,000 calories in a single workout, which requires replenishment in order to return to practice the next day prepared to compete.

"I would say that my breakfast and my lunch were too small. I wasn't eating enough. And when it came to dinner I was eating like seven plates. And it wasn't the best food, but I would just be eating three plates of the same food, just trying to get enough nutrition. And I found that even though I was eating so much, I wasn't gaining weight. Probably even my body was feeding off of my muscle mass and I was ending up just staying in a rut. I wasn't going above and competing at a higher level, so I had to adjust for that. I had to eat better, eat more and then I found myself gaining weight and building muscle and being able to compete at a higher level." -*Junior, Baseball*

Student-athletes are tempted (like other college students) to go for high fat, fast food choices, as a result of their demanding, fast-paced schedules. Unfortunately, not all campus-dining options offer choices with athletes in mind, although it is becoming more common for universities to offer more "health conscious" meal options. In addition to having quick access to "on the go" meals such as meal bars, yogurt, and fresh fruit, athletes should take the time to read the ingredients in the foods they consume. Processed foods should be kept to a minimum, as these foods are often high in preservatives, and do not provide a balance for long-term energy maintenance. Many athletic departments have access to sports nutritionists or as part of the resources available to student-athletes. If you are fortunate enough to have support in this area, make sure you take advantage of it!

Reflection Time:
- *What are the obstacles that keep you or could keep you from eating a well-balanced meal?*
- *What are three things that you can do to ensure that you are fueling your body appropriately for practice and competition?*

Sleep

How much sleep do you think you need daily? How much sleep do you receive? While there is some inconsistency around the exact amount of sleep experts believe student-athletes should receive on a daily basis, rest assured that you are most likely not receiving enough of it. For example, did you know that research suggests that adolescent athletes should receive at least nine hours of sleep a night (Sarchiapone et. al, 2014)? How many of you consistently slept that much in high school? Similarly, it would be optimal for collegiate student-athletes to receive between seven and eight hours of sleep nightly, though this is likely unrealistic given your obligations to your studies and sports (Moh, 2009; Costello, 2006). First-year student-athletes are often unaware of the physical and athletic benefits of adequate sleep.

35% of upperclass student-athletes reported that they rarely or never got 8 hours of sleep their first year.

Research suggests that limited sleep contributes to poor attention and focus, not just in the classroom but on the field as well (Jones & Harrison, 2001; Al-Sharman & Siengsukon, 2013; Jarraya, Jarraya, Chtourou, Souissi & Chamari, 2013). Athletes who fail to maintain appropriate amounts of sleep often find themselves lethargic, and experience difficulties managing frustration and disappointment in play. They have also been found to have greater challenges learning new skills or strategies. Poor sleep can decrease reaction time, which of course would present a significant negative

> "In college, it's very hard to go to sleep on time. Especially with all of the distractions going on. Like I said, you're on your own...so a mixture of sleeping and eating is definitely a great combination for high performance in athletics. Because you need that rest to run. You need it...because if you don't have it, it's going to drain you." *-Junior, Men's Track & Field*

impact, though more in some sports than others. Additionally, over time, a lack of sleep can contribute to psychological problems, including sustained stress, depression, and anxiety.

Sleep is essential to the solidification of learning; we know that sleeping after studying or learning new information helps us to retain that information at a higher rate (Leproult, Copinschi, Buxton, & VanCarter, 1997; Rasch, Buchel, Gais, & Born, 2007). This has a direct impact on performance in the classroom as well. Finally, sleep is essential to the healing and recovery process of your body, your immune system, and your muscles (Leproult, Van Reeth et al., 1997). As a first-year athlete, you are playing and practicing at a higher effort level than you have in the past; therefore, taking the time for optimal recovery for your body is important. Failing to place a high level of emphasis on your need for sleep will increase your risk of injury, decrease your ability to focus, and present an additional set of stressors that can be avoided.

---

7 Ways to Ensure Good Sleep

- Maintain a consistent sleep schedule. Try to go to bed around the same time every night.
- Create an optimal sleep environment. Complete darkness can often be a part of that, as light can impact the brain and the sleep cycle.
- Use earplugs, a fan, or a white noise machine to avoid loud noises that can startle and interrupt your sleep cycle.
- Turn off all electronic devices.
- Limit your number of naps. If you nap, make sure they are 20 minutes or less.
- Don't make major decisions immediately before bed.
- Avoid heavy meals, alcohol, caffeine and nicotine right before bed.

Reflection Time:
- *What are the things you need to do to make sure you get at least 7 hours of sleep each evening?*

Mental Prep

The level of competition in every sport dramatically increases as athletes move from high school to the collegiate level. College teams are a collection of the best high school athletes in the country. Therefore, the level of preparation (physical and mental) needed to perform at high levels changes for athletes as they transition from high school to college. Most athletes who are talented enough to compete in college are not required to focus and concentrate on their sport in high school in the same way that is

necessary at the college level. In high school, many of you were athletically superior to your competition, and could sometimes be successful by simply showing up and giving 100% effort. Unfortunately, the collegiate level is very different, and first-year athletes who are successful on the playing fields understand that they have to prepare themselves mentally for competition at this level. Yes, there may be some first-year athletes who can show up and play well in one game or practice, but those who are consistently the most successful on the field prepare themselves mentally for every practice and competition over the course of the season.

> "Games are completely different in college. You need to have your head on straight, you can't go in there thinking about your classes, about your social life, about anything. You need to go in and be focused. And I think that's a big thing that most freshmen don't have. And it takes your first two years to get that mindset. To be able to become a competitor and to challenge the limits of your mind and your body...to be able to be the best you can."
> *-Senior, Softball*

Mental preparation is vital for every athlete regardless of level, but it can be even more important for first-year college athletes because there are so many outside distractions and new situations that could negatively impact performance. While a focus on sport psychology or performance enhancement is beyond the scope of this text, there are a few mental skills that you can develop and practice that are tremendously effective. If you are interested in learning more about mental preparation for athletic performance, there are several resources listed in the resources section. Additionally, if you have access to a sport psychology consultant in your athletic department or on your campus, be certain to seek them out.

Visualization

Visualization is a practice that most athletes have been using in some form or another since they first began competing in sports. Your high school and club coaches may have encouraged you to sit quietly before a game or match and "envision yourself going out and playing well." This is the essence of visualization, and most elite athletes use this technique on a regular basis to improve their results. The reason that many athletes use this technique is because it works! There are a number of theories about why imagery works for athletes, but the bottom line is your brain sends signals to your muscles that mimic the messages sent when you are actually performing the task (Giuliam, et al., 2007; Lang, 1979; Wienberg & Gould, 2010). Each time we use visualization, our bodies increase the muscle memory of the images that we see in our minds. Therefore, when you practice your golf swing perfectly in your head prior to a tournament, your brain sends messages to the muscles in your body that would physically make that perfect golf swing happen. Then, when it comes time for you to go out on the course and make a perfect swing at the first tee, your body will be more ready to do it because it has practiced that swing countless times, both in reality and in your head.

---

9 Tips for Using Visualization

- Practice visualization for 5 minutes prior to every practice or competition.
- Try to visualize using more than one sense (smell, touch, sound, taste, sight).
- Picture the setting just as it will be during practice or game.
- Do not give up if you do not think it "works" right away. Practice makes perfect.
- Use both internal and external visualization.
- Control your images so you see yourself performing perfectly each and every time you use imagery.
- Do not end an imagery session without seeing yourself performing your task well. You do not want your body to remember a mistake prior to taking the field or court.
- Once you get good at using imagery, you will be able to slow down or rewind images in your head.
- Imagery can be a good practice for athletes who are injured, as research has found that it has helped athletes recover quicker and with less loss of skill as a result of being able to "practice" mentally.

Athletes who practice imagery effectively can do a few things really well. First, they are able to control their images. Going back to the golf example, imagery works best when golfers can imagine themselves performing their swing flawlessly. This is not as easy as it sounds, and some athletes struggle with imagery because they cannot control their images. If you are not perfect on your first few images, do not give up...it takes practice. Secondly, athletes who use this skill effectively can create both an internal and external view. An internal view is when athletes envision themselves performing their tasks like they would see it through their own eyes and is helpful when athletes want to visualize game strategy or how they will react in certain game situations. An external view is when athletes imagine themselves performing like they would see themselves on television or video and is useful when using visualization to help perfect a skill or technique. Athletes should use a combination of both internal and external visualization to get the most benefit from the practice. Obviously, in order to reap the benefits of visualization, you must use this practice in a very consistent and systematic fashion.

Think back to your most recent competition or practice. What can you create in your mind? Can you see yourself and others? Do you recall the sounds surrounding you? The audience, your coach or teammates, and things they may have said to you? Can you recall the smells? What about the way things felt? Depending on how you respond, you may have a greater ability to visualize using sight and smell, for example, than you do for some of the other senses. You can work to strengthen your ability in all of these areas.

Reflection Time:
- *How often and under what conditions do you use visualization?*
- *Can you use all senses (sight, sound, touch, smell and taste) while visualizing?*

Pre/post Competition Routines

As you are already witnessing, athletes who have been selected to play collegiate sports are physically gifted, and have been highly successful prior to coming to college. Continued success at a higher level of play requires a higher level of consistency and effort in both practice and competition. Great athletes and great students are not created by having one good game or doing well on one test, but rather by being able to replicate successful outcomes over time. While there may have been a way to obtain successful competition outcomes with minimal practice effort in high school, this is rarely the case on a collegiate level for at least two reasons. First, practicing at 70% may lead to a coaching decision that does not allow you an opportunity to compete. Secondly, your failure to practice and prepare at full effort on a daily basis puts you at a disadvantage in comparison to peers and competitors who bring that intensity on a consistent basis.

Creating pre and post-competition routines is another skill that helps many athletes prepare for and compete at a high level in both practice and games. Routines are different from rituals. Some athletes may wear the same socks or their lucky underwear for every game and believe that improves their performance, but a true pre/post-game routine is a series of events that an athlete does to feel more physically and mentally prepared. Typically, athletes know what they need to do in order to feel prepared for competition; unfortunately, we do not always *do* the things we know we need to do. One of the reasons we fail to do these things is because we have not purposefully created a "routine for success" for ourselves. We have not written down the process that works for us. We have not put much thought into the question...How do I put myself in the best possible position to be successful?

From the time we begin participating in sports (even at a young age), we sometimes become accustomed to practicing all week and crossing our fingers, "hoping" that we perform well in competitions. This pattern may not result in poor performance or other negative consequences when we are more physically gifted than the competition. However, at the collegiate level this mentality will not always work, and usually results in inconsistent performances. If we approach each practice and game with different thoughts and behaviors, we are likely to perform well for some competitions and not perform as well in others. Inconsistent thoughts and behaviors lead to inconsistent play on the field.

One way to combat this risk of inconsistent play is by creating a very detailed (but realistic) pre and post-competition routine that ensures your body is warmed up appropriately and puts you in the correct mind set to practice and compete with maximum intensity. How many basketball players use the first five minutes of a game to get "into the flow of the game", rather than enter into the game in that state of mind? Every minute in competition is valuable, and you do not have the luxury of using precious game time to warm up. So, what would it take for you to enter a competition "ready"? Many athletes struggle when they are asked to create a routine that they think will work for them, but the good news is that if you are competing at the collegiate level, you have already had a great deal of prior success. So, think back to the best two or three performances you had in your high school or club career. What did you do the night before the contest? What did you do an hour before the competition? What did you eat? How much sleep did you get? Did you take a nap? Did you do homework or read a book to take your mind off of the game? What did you do after the game? How did you analyze your performance?

Think about every detail of your most successful contest, and write down each detail that you think contributed to your successful performance. Take these factors and create a realistic pre/post game routine that you can follow regardless of where you are playing (home or away) and the time of day you are competing (early morning match or a night contest). A detailed pre/post competition routine can mentally and physically contribute to your ability to play consistently both in practice and games.

Emotion Regulation

Across every sport and level of competition, the ability to manage emotions and avoid feeling overwhelmed by internal or external pressures to perform is vital to success.

Most high performing athletes are able to manage their emotions effectively, recognizing their desire to win, but not allowing the pressured atmosphere surrounding high-level athletic events to hurt their performance. Conversely, athletes who cannot effectively manage that same stress typically have a difficult time performing consistently. Stress and anxiety cause muscle tension, and muscle tension restricts movement and overall speed. As a result, it can build up and make it virtually impossible to perform at a high level. In order to successfully navigate this challenge, athletes should understand how they typically respond to stress and practice stress reducing and coping techniques.

Not surprisingly, most athletes have experienced stress or even performance anxiety at some point during their careers. Performance anxiety is defined as stage fright, or fear, or apprehension that negatively impacts an activity or performance (Roland, 1997). For athletes to understand the source of their anxiety, it's helpful to determine if stress is the result of a natural tendency to become anxious (trait) or anxiety that is more situational—in this case, caused by participation in a sport (state). Trait and state anxiety have similar negative impacts on performance, but how an athlete manages these two forms of anxiety is quite different. Those who suffer from trait anxiety should search for the root cause of their stress, then work at eliminating or managing things in the environment that may contribute to their stress response. Athletes who are "naturally anxious" may find it helpful to work with a licensed therapist who specializes in working with athletes. These therapists understand anxiety from both a clinical and sports perspective, and they can offer practical strategies for managing this anxiety during competition.

Student-athletes who suffer from performance anxiety (state anxiety) must first understand and identify the source of the stress. This form of anxiety is often the result of an athlete's belief that the challenge in front of them may be greater than their current ability to perform or manage that challenge. Some athletes with performance anxiety become overwhelmed in competition or practice because they don't feel mentally or physically prepared. Think about it—it makes sense that you would be nervous to perform if you haven't studied your playbook or trained appropriately. Some athletes may become anxious during competition because they feel as though the stage is too big and the pressure associated with losing is too great. Injured athletes—or even athletes who have recovered from an injury—may experience sports-related anxiety because they feel that their bodies are not capable of performing at the necessary level. A lower confidence in one's abilities is generally at the root of performance anxiety for many first-year athletes.

For most individuals, anxiety related to competition is what we call "anticipatory" anxiety—the thoughts and worries that flood us before a situation or event. Once the event, performance, or competition begins, that anxiety level may drop or disappear completely. For others, anxiety can remain throughout the entire event, resulting in increased heart rate, loss of breath, hands shaking, tension, concentration difficulties, not being able to "shake off" mistakes, and ultimately, a decrease in performance. Rather than allowing your anxiety to control you, there are several ways that you can work to decrease your anxiety level in a competition situation.

8 Ways to Combat Performance Anxiety

- **Differentiate between "playing well" and winning**. Don't focus on the outcome. Focusing on winning increases the pressure you place on yourself and puts you in a "future" mindset. Instead, focus on those small things that you need to do that will allow you to perform well ("I know I need to focus on bringing my knees up in the last fifty meters," or "I need to make sure that I follow through with my shot"). Focusing on the small things will contribute to the likelihood of creating the outcome you want: winning.

- **Set realistic goals to improve specific skills**. Goals should be measurable, challenging and attainable. Vague goals such as "play well" do not offer much structure or direction. Similarly, you don't want them to be too easy. You want to have to work for them, but you also want them to be within your reach.

- **Reduce uncertainty by preparing for "worst case scenarios."** One of the biggest contributors to overwhelming performance anxiety is a lack of confidence, which can happen for a number of reasons—feeling unprepared or the fear of repeating a previous mistake, for example. One of the ways you can reduce uncertainty and increase the feeling of "being prepared" is to practice "worst case scenarios." Have a back-up warm-up that you can do relatively quickly in case you are ever short on time because things happen…buses break down, matches run late, meets run early.

- **Use "cue" statements to refocus.** Develop a 'cue' statement that you can practice as a means of helping you to regain your focus. A cue statement should be short, personal, and positive. It should be a short phrase that creates a visual image of the athlete you want to be, and allows you to return your focus and concentration to the task at hand.

- **Cognitive rehearsal and visualization**. Many athletes find that visualizing themselves successfully performing or completing a certain skill contributes to an increase in confidence, and therefore a decrease in anxiety. Cognitive rehearsal and visualization can both contribute toward feeling more prepared.

- **Positive self-talk.** You may surprise yourself to realize how often the dialogue in your head becomes negative when you make a mistake. Recognize critical self-talk and the mistakes or actions that trigger negative conversations with yourself, and work to challenge those automatic negative thoughts and make them positive.

- **Breathing.** This sounds like such a simple strategy, but it is one most often overlooked. Taking a deep breath during competition (or before certain moments—at the free throw line, for example, or before the race begins) can often be used as an opportunity to refocus and re-center. In the middle of stressful situations or when anxiety runs high, there is often the tendency to resort to shallow breathing, which leads to even more anxiety. Taking a deep breath may allow you a moment to use additional strategies (positive self-talk, cue statements, goal reminders) that can also decrease anxiety.

- **Prepare properly.** A significant contributing factor to performance anxiety may be the fear of being unprepared. If you feel confident in your preparation—for example, you know that you have taken practice seriously and consistently given your best effort—the result is often a significant level of confidence that you can "trust your training."

Creating coping mechanisms for managing stress and anxiety should be a part of most athletes' daily routine. This process may be even more important for a first-year student-athlete as there are so many opportunities to feel uncomfortable because of the new experiences and challenges. While there is definitely a benefit to the "good nerves" felt prior to competition or when approaching something new, failing to manage those same nerves can contribute to viewing play as a threat rather than an opportunity, and generate increased tension and poor performance.

Reflection Time:
- *How do you know when you are experiencing anxiety?*
- *What are situations or scenarios that may make you anxious?*
- *What are some ways that you manage your anxiety?*

Concentration

It should come as no surprise that athletes who consistently perform at a high level have a unique ability to concentrate solely on their immediate task. Regardless of whether it's in the weight room, at practice, or in competition, athletes who give complete effort and focus to the current task will perform better over the course of a season. You may find it difficult to concentrate appropriately on academic and athletic responsibilities because there are so many new experiences and opportunities for distraction that can contribute to underperformance.

In the sports arena, concentration is the ability to focus on the important information in your immediate environment, and the type and level of concentration necessary for optimal performance will differ based on the sport and the specific task at hand (Weinberg & Gould, 2011). When the environment changes rapidly, attention and focus must also change rapidly. If you are distracted by too many things—for example, the classroom assignment that you missed, the error you just made, worrying about whether you will get playing time this weekend, or thinking about the party after the game—you focus on the wrong performance related cues and make errors in performance. Since the connection between concentration and performance is so strong, it is helpful to be aware of your "normal" level of concentration, potential distractions, and methods to improve. Fortunately, concentration development, similar to muscle development, can be strengthened and improved over time. Below are a few ways athletes can increase their concentration levels to help improve performance. Keep in mind that the practice of mental skills is helpful in several different capacities; as a result, you may see some overlap across both athletics and academics.

---

5 Ways to Sharpen Concentration

- **Stay focused on the present.** Thinking too much about the past or the future creates anxiety; we have limited control over either and focusing solely on them serves as a distraction.
- **Engage in positive self-talk.**
- **Create a pre-competition routine.**
- **Use cue statements to refocus- both in practice and during competition.**
- **Over-learn skills.** Practicing certain skills repetitively allows them to become automatic in competition situations.

Goal Setting

Finally, the last "practical" tool to help you maximize performance during your first year as a college student-athlete is to engage in goal-setting activities. While most of you may have some general goals that you'd like to accomplish during your first year, both on and off of the field, you may not have the specifics worked out, or you may just have them "in your head". Goals are often likened to road maps; if we don't have them, and we are attempting to navigate new territory, there is absolutely no sense of where we are, or the direction we need to be going. It is also much easier to "get lost" without that road map.

Interestingly, it is not uncommon for the team to have goals, but for individual athletes to not really set them. Similarly, some athletes do actually take the time to establish goals at the beginning of the year, but then put them away and do not look at them again until the end of the year. Again, using the road map analogy, how helpful would it be to only consult your map at the beginning of your journey and again only at the end? Without regularly referring back to the map, you will have no way of knowing where you may have taken the wrong turn, you don't know where you're going, you can't make a plan for how to get there, and you will likely not even know when you reach your destination.

Think about some goals you would like to accomplish this year athletically. Once you have few objectives in mind, write them out. Section 3 in The College Survival Guide allows you to create academic, athletic, and social goals. Keep in mind that "good" goals require you to follow certain guidelines. The most commonly used method of describing good goals is by using the SMART method (Smith, 1994):

Goals should be **S**pecific. Remember, your goal is your road map, so if it's vague and not clear, it will not help you get anywhere. Your goals should also be **M**easurable: You need to be able to tell how close or far you are from success, which means there needs to be some metric or way of measuring your goal in your description of it. Is it the number of baskets I will shoot before and after practice? The number of minutes I will run every morning in addition to practice? The time I will spend studying math after class? Good goals are **A**ttainable: You want to make sure that your goals are something you can achieve. You want something that challenges you a bit, but is still within your reach. This requires you to be honest with yourself about your starting point as well. Your goals should be **R**ealistic: You want to make sure that the goals you set are within your control, and are possible. Finally, a good goal is **T**imely: You want to make sure that you have experiences of success along the way. It's hard to stay motivated if you set goals that are too far out into the future. Make sure that you have steps along the way where you can experience the taste of success. Setting timely goals also allows you to reevaluate them on a consistent basis, allowing you to adjust them according to how you are performing.

We often set outcome-oriented goals, such as "I want to get an A on my math test" or "I want to win the race tomorrow." Instead, focus more on process goals, since accomplishing these process goals will make it more likely that we can achieve our outcome goals. For example, if you want to get an A on your next math test, what do you need to do to get there? If you aren't doing very well right now, maybe you need to ask for assistance from your professor. Or set a goal of studying for at least 30 minutes every day. If you are successful in accomplishing these tasks, you make it more likely that you will earn an A on your math test. To just say "I want to earn an A" does not really help you create a plan to be successful.

Similarly, setting the goal of "winning the race" does not help you create a road map to get there; "win the race," means you would have to run faster than every runner out there. Unfortunately, that may not be realistic, and it is certainly not something that you can control. You need to set goals based on factors that are within your control. What would be the things you would need to do to put yourself in a position where winning the race is likely? You could set a goal of running every day for the next few months, and slowly building up your speed every week. There are two additional things you can do to increase your ability to accomplish your goals. The first is to share your goal with someone else. When we share our goals with those close to us, they can help us stay on track when we lose focus. The second action is to write it down. When goals are written down and posted in a place where you can see them frequently, it keeps them on your mind, and helps you make sure you are still on the right road.

> As a freshman, you have to get accustomed to competing against the best athletes in the world every week. So, keep your expectations in check, and set small goals instead of saying...I want to be the best now.
> –Senior, Women's Swimming

Athletic Identity and the Athletic Transition

Athletic identity is the degree to which you define yourself as an athlete (Brewer, Van Raalte, & Linder, 1993). Most college student-athletes have a very high athletic identity; the time that you have put into your sport, training, preparing, or even just thinking about it is in large part what has gotten you to where you are (Brewer & Cornelius, 2002). College coaches want student-athletes with high athletic identity. They know that you will be willing to put other things on the back burner in order to concentrate on performing to your highest potential on the court or field. You will value playing time, take practice seriously, and spend the necessary time in the weight room or training room to accomplish your athletic goals. High athletic identity is a positive quality, because it means that you are willing to do all of the difficult talks related to your sport. Think about it—athletic identity is something that has been accumulating since your first entry into sports. The first time you experienced success or received accolades and encouragement based on your athletic performance, it lit the fire that started your growth in this area.

So we know that those with a strong athletic identity are able to minimize distractions that take them away from focusing on their sport, and in most ways, strength in this area increases the likelihood for athletic success (Horton & Mack, 2000). However, there can also be a downside to strong athletic identity. Because of the desire to play as long and as much as you can, you may be less inclined to listen to your body, take a break, or rest when needed. You may have a great fear of missing out on athletic success, or you may over train, with the goal of giving yourself every athletic advantage possible. Research suggests that those with high athletic identity may be more likely to use performance-enhancing drugs, again as a result of wanting to gain any advantage that they can (Hughes & Coakley, 1991). High athletic identity may impact your definition of success, skewing it, or making it harder to recognize. You are also more likely to be negatively impacted by anything that may limit your chances to play. For example, injury may present a greater challenge and even contribute to emotional distress, as it can decrease playing time or cause perceived decreases in performance (Brewer, Cornelius, Stephan & Van Raalte, 2010).

---

3 Ways to Maintain Athletic Identity Balance

- **Work with your coaches to develop a realistic definition of success.** Strive to achieve and exceed that definition, but use it as a framework or a starting point.
- **Create balance in your life.** Make sure that you are setting and accomplishing goals in areas other than athletics.
- **Listen to your body.** We've already discussed the increased level of physical activity between high school and college athletics—recognize the difference between 'good pain' and 'bad pain.'

Don't compromise your values to obtain athletic success. Train and compete within the rules. Any success you gain, you want to gain it legitimately. While the gains of athletic success are higher at the collegiate level than they were in high school, the costs of breaking the rules are also greater, often with a lifelong impact.

Reflection Time:
- *What are some signs that may indicate that someone over-identifies with their role as an athlete?*

Mental Health Concerns in the Athletic Transition

Common psychological issues and diagnoses that impact student-athletes can contribute to or result from difficulties navigating the athletic transition. There is clearly a connection between mental health and athletic performance; while some conditions result from the desire or effort to improve performance, others stem from sports related disappointment. Listed below are some of the more commonly occurring diagnoses that we recognize in student-athletes as they manage the athletic transition. Keep in mind that if you are currently taking or considering taking any medication, make sure you share that information with your athletic trainer.

Adjustment disorders: There is actually a diagnosis that speaks to emotional or behavioral symptoms associated with the stressors of any major transition. Adjustment disorders are typically diagnosed when these behaviors occur within a three-month period of any major event, and may be accompanied with symptoms of anxiety or depression. One of the differences between "normal" adjustment and an adjustment disorder is the level of impairment that occurs in social, academic, or other areas of functioning. When the stress of leaving home, meeting new people, increased academic challenges and physical demands impair your ability to perform in your sport (or in the classroom or socially), you may meet the criteria for adjustment disorder. If you notice that it is difficult to concentrate in practice, find yourself struggling to perform consistently, attempt to avoid practice or meet your athletic obligations, it would be helpful to speak with someone about the multiple changes you have experienced in your transition to college.

Depression and/or depressive symptoms: Periodic sadness is a normal part of life; however, there are times when sadness seems to occur frequently, may increase in intensity, or may seem difficult to overcome. Symptoms that indicate a cause for concern about depression include sleeping too much or having difficulty sleeping, increased isolation, no longer enjoying experiences that used to be fun, difficulty concentrating or focusing, or increased fatigue. Depression can occur in first year student athletes when you find yourself disappointed in your current experience, particularly in comparison to what your expectations were. For example, realizing that the relationship with your coach is not as close as you thought it would be, finding it difficult to connect with new teammates, or receiving less playing time than you are accustomed to. Needless to say, there are many challenges that occur during your athletic transition that may contribute to depressive symptoms including

"Coming into college, you're around all of these athletes, you're battling to get attention, you're battling to get more scholarship money, you're battling to get on the track...to get attention at practice. With all of that pressure it would have been easy to get depressed. If I was feeling down, if I felt like I needed to get picked up, I would reach out to my support system. It was easy to find help in them, I just needed to believe in myself...and they would always remind me."-*Senior, Men's Track & Field* making the decision to redshirt, injury, coaching changes, etc. Simultaneously, fatigue, loss of motivation or enjoyment, difficulty sleeping, and other symptoms of depression can decrease your ability to perform athletically.

Anxiety related disorders: Anxiety related disorders are the most commonly experienced, as statistics indicate about 25% of the population will meet the criteria for an anxiety disorder at some point in their lives (Comer, 2011). Common anxiety disorders experienced among student-athletes include social anxiety disorder—a fear of being viewed negatively in social contexts—as well as post-traumatic stress disorder, which may occur following a traumatic event—and could even include an injury. A symptom of anxiety related disorders is "worrying thoughts," where there is significant concern or an overwhelming sense of dread or apprehension about what may happen in the future—for example, loss of playing time, scholarship, or poor performance. As you can imagine, when these thoughts occur too often, there is an increase in muscle tension, difficulty focusing on the task at hand, and eventually a decrease in performance.

Eating disorders and/or disordered eating: Earlier in this chapter, we discussed difficulties first-year student-athletes may experience around nutrition and the need to adjust eating habits when they begin competing at this level. Studies suggest that while sports participation typically does contribute to a healthier body image, in some cases, athletic participation may result in unhealthy or disordered eating patterns (Reinking & Alexander, 2005; Waldron, Stiles-Shipley, & Michalenok, 2001; Torres-McGehee, Monsma, Gay, Minton, & Mandy-Foster, 2011). Some first-year student-athletes may develop the misconception that weight loss will enhance athletic performance, and their limited nutritional knowledge may result in a loss of control or encourage the development of an unhealthy relationship with food. Shifts in eating behaviors that include a preoccupation with food, dieting, or weight loss, a decreased desire to eat in front of others, and rapid weight loss or frequent fluctuations in weight, may indicate the development of an eating disorder. While there might be a belief that weight loss will increase performance, especially in sports such as cross-country, diving, wrestling, and gymnastics, we know that optimal performance requires the consumption of enough calories to provide the energy necessary to practice and compete.

Common signs and symptoms of eating disorders include: a tendency to avoid eating in front of others, frequent trips to the bathroom after meals, misuse of laxatives or other diuretics, increasingly restricting diet and food choices, and frequently expressed unhappiness about weight and/or appearance. Eating disorders and *disordered eating* (because not everyone with unhealthy eating patterns will meet the full criteria for an eating disorder) similar to many of the other conditions discussed in this section are most successfully managed when they are addressed early in development. Recognizing these symptoms and intervening early is essential, especially because there is such a strong correlation between performance and eating behaviors, and our relationship with food is one with life long and life sustaining impact.

Substance use or related disorders: Substance use and other substance related disorders are the last category of mental health concerns that we will discuss, and this topic will be addressed more in depth in the next chapter. In many ways, substance use is a common occurrence among college students and student-athletes, almost so much that it is normalized in large part. While the use of alcohol and other substances may occur frequently with limited negative consequences for most college students, it has many detrimental athletic and academic implications for the student-athlete. Substance use may serve as a form of "self-medication," masking the presence of one of the other mental health issues introduced earlier and possibly contributing to the failure to recognize symptoms or seek help for depression or anxiety. Also, using substances such as alcohol, marijuana, or nicotine have a direct effect on physical well being; contributing to dehydration, loss of focus, lethargy, and decreased lung capacity, all side effects that will negatively effect athletic and academic performance outcomes.

Some student-athletes may use performance enhancing substances, stimulant prescription drugs, or even caffeine in an effort to improve or enhance their performance. Studies suggest a correlation between strong athletic identity (something we know is common among most individuals who are successful enough to be one of the few to become college student-athletes) and the willingness to consider using performance-enhancing drugs (Hughes & Coakley, 1991). Signs or symptoms that may indicate concerns around substance use would include increased use of any substance, possibly indicating a greater tolerance and requiring larger intake to receive the same results. Additional signs include difficulty in decreasing use of the substance when decreased use is a goal, increased irritability as a possible sign of withdrawal when the substance is not consumed, and hiding the use of a substance. Any or all of these behaviors can indicate that there may be a need to seek support or to intervene on the behalf of someone else. Early intervention may minimize the impact of what could develop into a lifelong struggle.

The mental health issues presented in this section can be related to numerous aspects of your athletic transition. For example, disordered eating behaviors or the use of performance enhancement substances can be the result of efforts to improve athletic performance while depression or anxiety may result from frustration or disappointment after failing to meet individual athletic performance goals. Urge teammates or other peers who are experiencing any of these symptoms to seek help, due to the risky nature of these problems.

Almost all universities provide on-campus counseling services free of charge to the entire student population. This is a great resource and can be a place to access a number of support options, including group and individual counseling and medication if needed. Many athletic departments also designate a specific person within the counseling center that can be a direct liaison for student-athletes; this individual usually has some athletic background or experience working specifically with student-athletes and can understand the challenges unique to this population. There are also an increasing number of athletic departments that have someone who works within the department to provide support for student-athletes around psychological and performance related concerns. Finally, you always have the option of accessing services outside of your university if you aren't comfortable with the idea of using services on campus. Regardless of where you choose to seek support, if support is necessary, it is crucial that you locate it and utilize it as early as possible.

International Students and the Athletic Transition

While many of the major transitions faced by international student-athletes may be related to cultural or language barriers, there are also some shifts that may be necessary to ease their athletic adjustment. International students make decisions about which university to attend based on a number of different factors. Some decide on a school because other student-athletes from their home country have encouraged them to attend; some have had the opportunity to interact with particular coaches during their high school athletic career; some may have been able to engage in an athletic event or competition at a particular university, while others have made the choice based on national ranking.

Similar to the different ways an international student-athlete decides to attend a university, their particular backgrounds and expectations will differ as well. They may have great expectations for significant playing time as a first-year student, or come in with the belief that they will receive greater support than they are provided. While in some ways, the athletic struggles associated with the experiences of first-year international student-athletes mirrors those of other first-year student-athletes, the distance from home, the limited social support, and the possible lack of integration into the team or larger university may accumulate to have an even greater negative impact. There are some suggestions we can offer that may help to navigate the athletic transitions in the first year for international student-athletes.

---

4 Ways for International Student-Athletes to Adjust Athletically

- **If there is a language barrier, continue to build your language skills.** The sooner you feel confident in your ability to communicate with coaches, teammates, and trainers, the sooner you will feel connected and integrated into the team.

- **Learn about the cultures of your coaches and teammates**. Taking interest in the cultures of those around you will illustrate a willingness to invest in your team. When you demonstrate this willingness, others will usually work hard to learn about your culture as well and this mutual connection can increase team cohesion and success.

- **Continue to strengthen the relationship with the coach who recruited you.** This relationship can be an additional source of support. Usually, the coach who played a part in bringing you onto campus is tremendously invested in your success, and is willing to serve as a sort of "cultural translator" in your adjustment experience. They may be able to provide insight, offer you honest feedback, and help you develop the skills necessary to thrive in that environment.

- **Be open to the differences in style of play and coaching philosophies if they differ from what you are accustomed to**. For some student-athletes, and in some sports, there may be significant differences between the approach that coaches take, or even the style and level of play required. Beginning the year with an open mind despite these new tactics will allow you to trust your training and increase your likelihood for success.

Transfer Students and the Athletic Transition

While much of the content in this chapter is directed toward first-year student-athletes, we are also aware that the first year for transfer student-athletes can present quite an adjustment. Although similar in some ways to the transition for other first-year athletes, depending on the situation that led to your decision to transfer, the adjustment process may be different. In comparison to true freshmen, transfer students often come in with more experience and exposure. You may be more aware of the challenges associated with balancing academics and athletics. You have already had interactions with college coaching, the increased level of practice and play, and the effort necessary to develop positive relationships with teammates and coaches. In many ways, you are more knowledgeable about what it takes to succeed at the collegiate level. As a result, it is important to work to leverage that experience to your benefit.

7 Ways to Leverage the Transfer Student Athletic Experience

- **Don't let the past dictate your future.** Some of you may be entering your new institution with preconceptions based on experiences on your old campus. Learn from the past, but remain open-minded, and don't allow your past to interfere with this new opportunity.

- **Entrench yourself with your teammates.** Throw yourself into your team, working hard to become integrated. Unlike your first-year peers, as a transfer student, you may not have the same amount of time to build relationships with teammates and will have to make a greater effort to connect with them.

- **Consider living on campus or with other teammates.** Building relationships with the team members you will have the most contact with—those in your position, or who compete in your event with you may be beneficial.

- **Come to campus over the summer to get acclimated to your teammates and coaches.** Deciding to remain on campus over the summer gives you more time and access to develop those important relationships.

- **Build study groups with teammates in your major or classes.** Take advantage of all opportunities to engage with teammates beyond just your athletic activities.

- **Work to build positive relationships with your new coaches.** Keep in mind that you have to play "catch up" with your new coaches. Philosophies, team strategies, and overall coaching styles will be different from your previous team. Interact with your new coaches to learn these as quickly as possible.

- **Do a self-assessment.** Reflect on what you did well and areas of improvement from your previous experience. Integrating this information into your current athletic situation will contribute to a positive adjustment and increase the likelihood for success at your new institution.

Depending on the circumstances that led to the decision to transfer, many student-athletes in this position may feel that they are at an academic and athletic disadvantage when compared to their first-year or upperclassmen peers. Not only are you in the position of having to learn another campus, community, team, and style of play, you may also be coming in with preconceived ideas or expectations that can serve as distractions or barriers to a positive transition. While there is no one way to alleviate the potential difficulties that you may experience as part of the adjustment process, there are ways to increase the likelihood that you are able to use your previous experiences to your advantage.

> **"I picked the wrong school my first time. I loved my individual coach, but the team atmosphere was horrible. I think as a transfer, meshing is the most important thing. But if you know the team, like I do now…and like them, you're going to want to throw further or run faster because the team is behind you. Because you are part of a family. -*Senior, Women's Track & Field***

Discussion Questions

1. What has been the greatest challenge for you athletically during your first-year?

2. What are two major differences between your high school coaches and teammates and your college coaches and teammates?

3. What are four or five actions that you take to ensure that you perform at a high level athletically?

4. What type of coaching style do you feel motivates you to perform at your best? Please explain.

Journal Space

_____

_____

_____

_____

_____

_____

_____

_____

_____

Chapter 3:
The Social/Cultural Transition

While many athletes expect a challenging athletic transition when they move from high school to college, they often find the social and cultural transition to be just as daunting. The transition that you are making socially is not much different from that of other first-year college students. There are a number of things in your social life that will change (or may remain the same) depending on what your experience was like in high school. For some of you, college may present you with the first opportunity to interact with, compete with, or live with people who differ from you racially, religiously, culturally, or in their sexual orientation. To get the most out of the college experience and to optimize team performance, it is imperative that you embrace those differences and develop close relationships.

All first-year students are faced with the challenge of adjusting; however, the spotlight effect on college athletics increases pressure on student-athletes to adjust quickly to their new environment (Humphrey et al., 2000; Papanikolaou et al., 2003; Wilson & Prithcard, 2005). For most colleges and universities, the athletic arena plays a central role in the social life of the campus as well as in the larger community. Consequently, a mistake made during that transitional time not only impacts the student-athlete, but depending on the severity of the error, there are possible implications for the athletic department, the team, and the university as a whole. While the social and cultural adjustments span multiple areas, we have divided them into three primary categories: diversity, decision-making, and interpersonal dynamics.

> **12% of upperclass student-athletes felt that their race played a role in how they were treated during their first year.**

Diversity

Many groups define the term "diversity" differently, but for the purposes of this text, we define diversity as a fusion of multiple elements or qualities (Merriam Webster, 2013). In other words, diversity is a combination of all of the different characteristics that make us unique. Despite your background, beliefs, or perspective, there is a need to acknowledge and respect all individuals, regardless of differences. Here are a few questions to consider: What is your racial background? How do you define diversity? How diverse was your high school? What about your friendship group? What are some of the stereotypes that you may have about other groups? Would you feel comfortable with a roommate who comes from a different religious background? Is your campus 'disability friendly'? Do you feel welcome in all areas of campus?

For many students, college is a time when you are faced with a shift in the diversity of your environment. While this can present a significant challenge for some students, it does not serve as a challenge for all. For example, if you enter college from a very racially diverse high school, you may be comfortable sharing a room with a student from a different race or ethnicity. Similarly, it is possible to have attended a racially diverse high school, but have had little to no interaction with individuals different from yourself; this can make it uncomfortable to interact closely with someone you view as different. In contrast, coming from a homogenous environment, where most people share similar backgrounds, you may find it difficult to adjust to a college campus where you are surrounded by faces and cultural practices that may be outside of your comfort zone. Despite the racial makeup of the environment that you come from, you will benefit from embracing the diversity and varied perspectives that come from those racial and ethnic differences.

> "One thing I would say is that in college, have an open mind. Because you're going to be around people with a lot of different personalities, and you probably are not going to see many of the same people on a day to day basis."
> *-Junior, Women's Golf*

Most universities promote the concept of "diversity", but this means different things for different people. For most institutions, there is a desire to ensure that all groups feel comfortable across campus regardless of race, religion, sexual orientation, socioeconomic status, or physical disability. However, it can be quite a difficult task to ensure that all students experience this sense of inclusion, especially on a large campus. Research consistently demonstrates that a diverse environment contributes to a higher level of learning for all students, student-athletes included (Hurtado, Milem, Clayton-Pedersen & Allen, 1998, 1999; Chang, 1999; American Council on Education & American Association of University Professors, 2000; Gurin, Dey, Hurtado & Gurin, 2002). In spite of a diverse environment, many first-year students are apprehensive about interacting with those they feel are different from them, and may isolate themselves or shut themselves off from learning from the multiple perspectives that this type of environment offers. To benefit from the value that diversity can bring, there is a need for openness and a willingness to learn.

Student-athletes have the ability to self-segregate more than most groups of students (Pinkerton, Hinz & Barrow, 1989). One of the great things about being a first-year student-athlete is that there is a ready-made support group present- an advantage that few students have. Most first-year students worry about creating new friendships as they adjust to college. We often see roommates stick together, attending meals and social events with each other or other people who live on the same floor or in the same dorm. Student-athletes have teammates they can depend on for friendship, so they do not have to navigate these new friendships if they do not want to. However, the disadvantage for first-year student-athletes may be isolation from the larger social system; they may remain segregated and miss out on the growth that can result from being exposed to a wider range of individuals.

It is not uncommon for students who identify themselves as minorities to feel marginalized on some college campuses (Cabrera, Nora, Terenzini, Pascarella & Hagedorn, 1999; Ancis, Sedlacek & Mohr, 2000). These students may not feel the sense of ownership or connection to really become integrated into the school, utilize resources, or interact with others, making it difficult to find a fit on campus. One thing to keep in mind is that we all have multiple aspects of identity. For example, while you may be in the racial *minority* on your campus, you may be in the religious *majority*. Or you may identify with a *minority* group around sexual orientation, but in the *majority* in terms of physical ability. Conversely, you may be in the *majority* in terms of physical or visible ability, but may struggle with an "invisible" disability such as dyslexia, which may present an additional factor to navigate. The point is, try not to allow the aspect of your identity that you view as "minority" to interfere with your decision to get involved, to use the resources available to you, and to connect with others.

Numerous college student-athletes report that they have experienced some discrimination or prejudice as a result of carrying the "athlete" label (Engstrom & Sedlacek, 1991; Bruening, Armstrong & Pastore, 2005; Comeaux, 2012). They share that professors and/or other students often believe stereotypes about student-athletes and fear that theymay be treated differently as a result. Stereotypes can be detrimental; they do not allow you to get to know people on an individual basis and can also lead to discriminatory actions and treating others unfairly.

During their first year, 8% of upperclass student-athletes felt that their professors treated them poorly because they were an athlete.

Similar to the stereotypes that others may have about student-athletes, you may harbor stereotypes about other groups. Consider common stereotypes about different groups, and jot down the first things to come to mind. Then, think about specific challenges to those stereotypes based on the real interactions you have had with members of those groups. An example is provided for you in the first row.

Group	Stereotype	Reality
Student–athletes	Dumb jocks, not interested in learning, lazy	Hard working, disciplined, focused

Religious Diversity

In the past, religion has been considered a "private matter" on most campuses. However, research indicates that there has actually been an increased focus and integration of religion and religious diversity in the university setting (Lee, 2002). While there is greater acceptance of religious differences on many college campuses, evidenced by campus programming and events, religious holiday acknowledgements, areas of study and student groups, there remains a stronger emphasis on some religions as compared to others. As a result, students may have differing degrees of comfort with religious variation. One of the most significant benefits of being a college student is the amount of diversity, opportunities for exposure, and learning that occurs from hearing multiple perspectives. Although it is certainly easy to limit yourself by remaining in the same social group, there is much to be said for expanding that group as well.

Similarly, as a first-year student-athlete, you may also have some preconceived notions about how your teammates will view you based on your religious background, experiences, or conviction. As a new team member, you could have some apprehension about how you will fit in with the rest of your team if they do not share similar views or understand your perspective; there may be fear of alienation by teammates, or concern that it may present a barrier, limiting connections and the possibility of building relationships. Unfortunately, this can become a self-fulfilling prophecy, where the fear does create a barrier, and you isolate yourself, preventing peers and teammates from getting to know you. Rather than allowing your religious differences to be a barrier to relationships, use these opportunities to learn, grow, and develop an inclusive perspective that is necessary for success in our increasingly diverse world. Here are some ways to learn from the religious diversity around you and expand the viewpoint of those you interact with as well:

---

6 Ways to Understand Religious Diversity

- Ask questions and share experiences.
- Attend a religious service or worship with a denomination that is different from your own.
- Get involved in the religious student groups on campus or in the community.
- Be willing to invite teammates to religious services, if they express interest.
- Challenge teammates when they make stereotypical or discriminatory comments about religions or religious individuals.
- Take a class in the religion department.

Sexual Orientation

Most discussions of diversity focus primarily on race and gender, and the goal is usually one of inclusion and equality. There are additional aspects of diversity that may be less obvious and acknowledged less frequently. Historically, one area of discomfort has been the realm of sexual orientation. Research indicates that as images of sexual diversity become popular in the media and issues around sexual orientation are addressed in the political sphere, people are becoming more comfortable discussing their sexual preferences and are more accepting of others who differ in sexual orientation (Frankowski et. al, 2004). While there has been an increase in openness and a focus on inclusion within the larger society, unfortunately the world of athletics—at both the collegiate and professional levels—is one of the last realms to embrace this shift. In many ways, there remains tremendous fear of discrimination, bullying, and exclusion where sexual orientation and athletics intersect.

As the NCAA guidelines state, everyone benefits from a climate of "respect and inclusion," not just those who identify as LGBTQ (lesbian, gay, bisexual, transgendered, queer/questioning) or embody other aspects of diversity (Griffin & Hudson, 2013). In the true essence of team-work and inclusivity, teammates with differing beliefs and lifestyles can work together to achieve a common goal and develop positive relationships on and off the field. This requires you to be open minded, willing to listen and learn from others about their experiences and beliefs, and respectful of differences. At the end of the day, we all have more similarities than we have differences,

> 10% of upperclass student-athletes felt that during their first year, they were treated poorly by students (non-athletes) because they were athletes.

and the more diverse an environment is, the more we all gain. Listed below are ways in which you can work to be more inclusive around issues of sexual orientation.

---

6 Ways to Embrace Diversity around Sexual Orientation

- **Be mindful of automatic assumptions.** While some aspects of diversity are more obvious, sexual orientation is one that can be more "invisible." Making assumptions about someone's sexuality may result in regrettable actions.

- **Language matters**. Using terms like "That's so gay," "no homo," or other derogatory statements—though trendy and popular locker room talk—suggests that you may not be accepting or supportive.

- **Challenge the assumptions and language of others.** Speak out when you hear offensive or demeaning language. Remember, everyone benefits from a climate of respect and inclusion. Your decision to speak out in support of someone may encourage others to be more open.

- **Don't change the relationship.** If someone is comfortable sharing their sexual orientation with you, don't alter your relationship with them. The decision to disclose this information can be a difficult decision to make. It serves as an indicator of trust, and there may be a fear that this disclosure will result in rejection or the loss of a relationship. For example, deciding that you are uncomfortable in the locker room after a teammate discloses their sexuality to you may send a message that the relationship has changed.

- **Don't "out" someone else.** Again, the decision to disclose sexual orientation can be a major milestone, and it may not be information they would choose to share with everyone. Don't make the automatic assumption that because they've shared this information with you, they want others to know.

- **Don't allow your differences to impact team performance.** While it is possible that you will not agree with the lifestyle choices of every member of your team, it is nonetheless necessary for team success that you are able to work together effectively. Don't let the differences that exist off the field negatively impact how you play and work together on the field.

Ability

The concept of physical or mental ability as an aspect of diversity may present a shift in viewpoint for some. This relates to the notion of visible and invisible differences, and there may be varying degrees of comfort around differences in level of ability. In some environments, those who have physical or mental disabilities may be marginalized or hidden from public view. Some high schools isolate these students in special classrooms, where they are separated from the rest of the student population. As a result, you may have had limited experiences interacting with students with very visible physical disabilities—moving from class to class in a wheelchair, for example, or the complex muscle movements of someone with cerebral palsy. You may also have limited experience with those who must navigate the difficult "invisible" disabilities, such as autistic spectrum disorders or other mental health related concerns. However, as the availability of resources increases and advances in technology occur, higher education is becoming more accessible to all students, across all ability levels.

Again, to contribute to a climate of respect and inclusion for all students, there is a need to be increasingly open-minded. Society's tendency is to either avoid or become hyper-focused on those individuals with visible physical disabilities, thus leading to the belief that these individuals don't fit, or that they don't exist. Rather than continue this pattern of interaction, take the time to include these individuals into the larger campus community, to the degree that you can. Treat them as you would any other peer, basing your relationship with them on actual interactions rather than stereotypes or assumptions. Additionally, there are less visible aspects of ability—most often connected to mental health related issues—that may be another challenging area to navigate. We will speak more specifically to mental health related abilities later in this chapter.

Echoing previous content, be mindful of language, both yours and the language of those around you, and work to challenge dismissive or demeaning statements that others may make. Remember, your goal is to help create a respectful and inclusive campus community for all.

Decision-Making

This section of the chapter, but perhaps the most important, examines the decision-making process and interpersonal dynamics. There are both advantages and disadvantages related to the lack of structure, freedom, and new opportunities that a college experience provides. Learning to navigate relationships with roommates, teammates, and new coaches requires not only an ability to understand others, but also a certain degree of self-awareness. It is important that you understand your emotional triggers and how your response to them plays a role in your decision-making

27% of upperclass student-athletes reported engaging in behaviors that their parents and coaches wouldn't approve of during their first year.

process in every area, from the choices you make on a Saturday night, to financial choices, to your ability to be negatively influenced by peer pressure. Emotional awareness and better decision-making will allow you to thrive socially, develop positive relationships, and present you with opportunities that can set the stage for future success.

We are often faced with choices in college that we did not have to face or were sheltered from in high school, and making poor choices during those earlier years posed limited threat for long term negative impact. College student-athletes, especially first-year student-athletes, often have more supervision than their non-athlete peers, which may create a false sense of security or safety. For example, non-athletes and athletes alike are typically held accountable for their behaviors by their residential staff, professors, and roommates, while student-athletes are also held accountable by their coaches, athletic academic advisors, and upper-class teammates. Despite the presence of these individuals of influence, there is still significantly more opportunity for poor decision-making due to the increased freedom that college provides. Additionally, most college students want to fit in with their peers and may be willing to do things that they would not choose to do in high school, making poor choices that can sometimes lead to dire consequences. Avoiding these pitfalls requires you to gain additional awareness of factors that can contribute to your poor decision-making and develop skills that will allow you to communicate your choices and needs effectively with others.

---

8 Common Social Challenges Experienced by College Student-Athletes
- Poor time management
- Alcohol/substance use
- Hazing
- Poor financial decisions
- Managing peer pressure
- New sexual experiences
- Mismanaging social media
- Failure to ask for help

In the following section several of these areas will be discussed, along with tools and techniques to help you manage the temptation to be distracted by these barriers. We begin the section discussing emotional intelligence and communication skills, both of which provide the foundation for good decision making and building positive relationships. The remainder of the section addresses some of the major social areas that first-year student-athletes find themselves having to navigate; these areas can include poor decision making, building unhealthy or ineffective relationships, and failure to communicate with others in a direct and respectful manner. Tools for strengthening your skill set in these areas will also be provided in the College Survival Guide, including financial management worksheets aimed at helping you make good decisions regarding money.

Reflection Time:

- *What are two or three unhealthy decisions that first-year students can make that may have a long term negative impacts on their overall college experience?*

Emotional Intelligence

Understanding yourself and how you respond to and interact with others has significant implications for your ability to be successful in every area of your life, particularly social interactions and relationship development. How well do you manage your emotions? Are you able to tell when you're stressed? Frustrated? Angry? How do you demonstrate those emotions? Would anyone watching be able to tell? How well can you assess and understand the emotions of others? Have you ever just "lost it" in a competition or practice, and you wished you had been able to "keep it together"? These questions all examine a concept commonly known as *emotional intelligence*, and while it's not one of the most common forms of intelligence that we measure in school, we know that it plays an important role in the lives of high-level athletes. Emotional intelligence is defined as a combination of self-mastery plus social intelligence (Goleman, Boyatzis & McKee, 2002). Further explained, self-mastery is the degree to which you know yourself, and your ability to regulate your emotions across contexts. Social intelligence is defined as your social skill set: can you empathize with others or take the perspective of someone else?

Emotional intelligence is composed of five components: self-awareness, self-regulation, social skill, empathy, and motivation (Goleman, 1998). Emotional intelligence (or Emotional Quotient better known as **EQ**) requires the ability to identify both your own emotions and the emotions of others accurately, the ability to express your emotions clearly, and the ability to regulate your emotions as well as the emotions of those around you. Think about each of these areas. Why do you think this ability plays a significant role in not just athletic achievement and success but also in navigating the college experience?

There are many debates about the source of emotional intelligence: are we are born with it (similar to our IQ) or is it something we can develop and strengthen, as with other mental skills? There is certainly a connection between emotional intelligence and self-confidence, and we know that self-confidence contributes to performance outcomes. The College Survival Guide in Part II includes an exercise to further examine the concept of emotional intelligence and help you to develop self-awareness around each of the five components.

---

5 Benefits of High Emotional Intelligence

- You know how to motivate yourself for peak performance.
- You can support your teammates and provide positive feedback as well as constructive criticism and encouragement.
- You can help manage conflict within the team.
- You can change your thinking to create the emotion you need.
- You can better "bounce back" from mistakes, rather than becoming consumed by them.

Communication Skills

A key component of enhancing your social development is being able to communicate effectively. Similar to emotional intelligence, gaining self-awareness about your communication patterns and the ways others communicate will increase your likelihood of building healthy relationships. Throughout the text we have discussed the importance of building positive relationships with teammates, coaches, roommates, other students on campus, and professors. In Chapter 1, we discussed the DiSC® profile, which is often used by many college teams to allow teammates—and coaches—to better understand each other. While in some ways the DiSC® does allow greater understanding and self-awareness related to the ways we typically interact with others, it does not necessarily provide us with a means of assessing our most natural style of communication.

Although the specific details will vary depending on the situation and nature of the relationship, there are four predominate styles used in day-to-day communication, and it can be helpful to be aware of yours as you work to build relationships throughout your college experience and beyond. It is also important that you are able to identify or understand the communication patterns of those in your environment to allow you to work better with others and increase goal accomplishment.

There are four primary communication styles: passive, aggressive, passive-aggressive, and assertive (Covey, 1989; Van Dijk, 2011). Individuals who tend to communicate in a *passive* manner often hide their emotions from others and even themselves in many ways. They may have a fear of hurting, disappointing, or angering others, and consequently may feel that it is easier to suppress their emotions rather than speak up and have their needs met. These individuals will likely avoid conflict and may run the risk of being taken advantage of in certain situations. In contrast, individuals with an *aggressive* style of communicating may be forceful or demanding of others. They may be seen as intense and likely to challenge others, even when it is inappropriate to the particular situation. In extreme cases, aggressive individuals may be feared by others and can have difficulty maintaining honest and healthy relationships.

Passive-aggressive communication styles are identified by mixed messages. Individuals who communicate this way tend to express themselves more nonverbally, in body language that contradicts what they verbalize, or they may use sarcasm and other subtle methods of communicating their emotions. This form of communication often leaves individuals unhappy, unable to communicate their feelings to others or get their needs met. Finally, an *assertive* style of communication is considered the healthiest method, as individuals who communicate this way are often concerned about both their own needs as well as the needs of others. Those who use a predominately assertive style are likely to be direct, clearly articulating their thoughts and emotions while simultaneously respecting the thoughts and feelings of others. People who communicate in this manner are likely to be placed in positions of leadership, as they are relied upon to help others work together effectively.

As you navigate the reminder of this section, you will begin to understand how communication skills can play an important role in all aspects of your life. For example, effective time management requires you to be able to communicate to others your priorities, explain your choices, and in some cases, learn to say no. Similarly, avoiding negative consequences of hazing and interpersonal violence, maintaining positive sexual health, and making good social media choices all depend on your ability to communicate effectively. In the College Survival Guide, we introduce a framework from where you can gain awareness of the ways in which you interact with others based on those four styles. You can use this knowledge to further develop your communication skill set and to enhance your relationships with others.

Time Management

One of the factors of college life that many first-year college students have to become accustomed to is the lack of supervision, the abundance of unstructured time, and the increase in negative consequences that can result when one or both of these areas is mismanaged. For most first-year students (athletes or non-athletes), high school was a time when your parents or care givers were pretty aware of where you were and what you were doing. While there may have been free time, because of the adult supervision, there was a consistent expectation that things like studying and attending class were required.

> "You have to prioritize and you're not an athlete-student, you're a student-athlete, so you have to. I feel like I was just juggling. It was a juggling act the whole year. I didn't eat lunch, because I felt like I didn't have time, so you have to make sure you're staying healthy, and on top of your school work. Sometimes I think, if you didn't have to sleep, it would be so much less stressful. But, all-nighters are not good because you're just stressed out the next day. You sleep through your alarm and you start all over again." *-Junior, Women's Tennis*

As a result, the amount of damage that could potentially occur as a result of skipping classes or choosing not to do homework was somewhat minimized. However, some students come from households where they were the ones who essentially regulated themselves; maybe parents or caregivers were juggling full-time work, or birth order (particularly for oldest children) put them in a position where they were the ones carrying the responsibility for themselves and younger siblings. Thus, freshman year may be the first time you are faced with the need to independently manage your time with high stakes consequences attached to those decisions.

In high school, were you typically late, either to events or completing and handing in assignments? Were you often early to class or quick to begin an assignment right after it was assigned? Having some awareness of how you may have operated in the past will help you create a time management plan to contribute to your success in college. Depending on your background, you may find the concept of time to be more fluid, or you may view time more rigidly. For example, in some cultures when a time is set for an event it is simply a suggestion, while for others there is a tremendous cost related to being late. Similarly, some of you may be very detail oriented, and come from environments that have a tendency to write everything down, become 'super scheduled', and never take the risk of a task remaining undone, or being late for something. To determine how to best manage your time, you need to think about your individual background, and how you will need to adapt to the time requirements of your current environment – which in college tends to be relatively strict.

Lack of supervision can impact multiple areas of the first-year college experience, ranging from simple time

> "Being in college and having the independence is hard, because in high school, I had my mother over my back. She made sure I had good grades and made sure I was studying. When you're living at home with your parents it's a lot easier, but when you go off to college, it's a lot easier to procrastinate. Whether it was video games, watching TV, hanging out with my friends, putting a lot of focus into a relationship. That was really where I struggled in my first year because I focused so much on everything else, that school was hard to get adjusted to...being that free." *-Sophomore, Football*

> "If you can stick to a schedule in college, it's a whole lot easier to get things done. Especially being a college athlete... most college students can get by because they have a lot of free time. People don't understand how much time athletics takes up...practice time, recovery, training room and games..."
> *-Sophomore, Men's Basketball*

management difficulties to more complex poor decision-making. Although this seems like a simple concept, poor time management can be the downfall of any first-year college student. While some may believe time management to be an academic issue, it is really one that includes all aspects of the college experience. Most universities spend a great deal of time, energy, and financial resources introducing first-year students to the numerous ways of becoming involved, and research indicates that the more socially integrated a college student is, the greater likelihood of retention and successful navigation of the first-year (Tinto, 1999; Swail, 2004). For student-athletes, this level of enticement can lead to over commitment, where they have a difficult time balancing the multiple demands of academics, athletics, social life, and multiple campus activities.

Most student-athletes acknowledge that their commitment to sports in high school actually contributed to effective time management, as they were constantly aware of the need to balance their academic requirements with sport. For example, if they knew they would be out of town, or have to travel for athletics, many high school athletes felt compelled to work ahead and get their assignments completed early so they could maintain their athletic and academic balance. Since research tells us that high school student-athletes are more likely to graduate high school than those students who aren't athletes, we can assume that this balancing act is successful (McCarthy, 2000; Bowen & Green, 2012). However, unlike high school, college student schedules are much more flexible; students spend less time in class and less time with someone standing over their shoulders, reminding them that they need to do their homework or study for an exam. The increase in flexibility can sometimes lead to the mistaken belief that there is more time to complete tasks, enjoy roommates and friends, and complete classwork with little to no negative cost to student-athletes. Unfortunately, this is rarely the case, and student-athletes, whose ability to remain eligible to compete athletically relies upon their academic success,

> "During my freshman year, I was trying to discover how to say no, and figure out if my athletics meant more to me than partying with the people in my dorm. And as a collegiate athlete, you have more influence. And being that school's face...you have to know that partying isn't all of who you are and you either chose athletics or you chose that life. Because you can't have both. You can't...no one can do all of that and still be successful...or as successful as they would want to be." *-Senior, Men's Soccer*

can often pay a higher price for poor time management than students who are not athletes.

Effective time management requires us to prioritize and focus on the things that are of greatest importance to us. For example, while academic requirements such as study hall, independent studying, homework assignments, and exam prep are essential to prioritize, so are things we often take for granted such as eating and sleeping. These last two tasks are especially important for college student-athletes as both nutrition and rest significantly impact performance on the field. This may mean that you have to sit down and create a list, ranking in order of importance those things that you must accomplish. Once you have some idea of those tasks in order and a realistic assessment of how much time they will require, you are able to draw out a schedule and give yourself ample time to successfully manage them.

All first-year students have to create some kind of timetable for the academic and social demands that they must navigate; how much time they need to allot to study for the math exam on Friday, or how long it will take to write the paper that is due in the middle of the semester. Student-athletes, however, have the additional athletic demands to add to their master schedule. How might your schedule shift during pre-season and in-season? When is the best time for you to take a lunch break on days that you may lift weights or have practice twice during the day, as compared to the days with only one scheduled practice? While it is important to include "fun" things on your priority list, it is essential to create some balance between the "want to's" and the "have to's," ensuring that you tackle those things that "have to" get done before the more enjoyable tasks.

List five things that you **have to do** next week, and rate them in level of importance (**High**, **Medium**, or **Low**).

What are two or three things that you **want to do** that can serve as a mental or physical break?

Task	Level of Importance (H,M,L)	Due Date or Timeline

Many high school students maintained some sort of agenda to help them manage their busy schedules; due to the decrease of structure in college it can be even more important for student-athletes to manage their demands more effectively. One of the best ways of managing your time is to maintain an agenda and create a schedule for the entire semester that includes due dates for assignments, scheduled times for practice or competitions, travel days, and the dates for any other activities or commitments you have. Most classes typically hand out a syllabus for the entire semester at some point during the first week of class. This syllabus serves as your contract, reminding you of when all assignments are due, and the dates of exams. Sit down with your calendar or agenda, your practice and competition schedule for the semester, and your syllabus for each class, and mark down the important dates and corresponding assessments and tasks.

It is also important to check your agenda daily; it is counterproductive to write everything down without making sure that you take the time to check it consistently to see where you need to be, or to update it if and when things change. This proactive approach will allow you to know what to expect, and when to expect it, which enables you to be prepared rather than surprised. For example, integrating your syllabus into your calendar makes it less likely that you will forget there is a test scheduled and walk into class unprepared. Compiling these sources of information also gives you the opportunity to inform your professors when you may be out of town for athletic events and potentially miss a class, assignment, or exam. Not only does this approach help you better manage your schedule and increase your potential for success, it also sends a message to your professor that you are serious about academics and that you want to do well.

The College Survival Guide includes a copy of a daily schedule that you can use to help you organize and manage your time, as well as directions on how you can most effectively use it.

10 Ways to Effectively Manage Your Time

- **Make a "to do" list.**

- **Check your list daily to make sure you are getting things accomplished.**

- **Establish deadlines for your tasks.** Often we keep moving things from one to do list to the next. Set a deadline to ensure that you accomplish your tasks in a timely fashion.

- **Minimize multitasking**. Research shows that multitasking actually contributes to more errors as compared to completing tasks one by one (Sanbonmatsu, Strayer, & Medeiros-Ward, Watson, 2013; Bredemeier & Simons, 2012).

- **Prioritize your tasks, and complete the most pressing tasks first.**

- **Reward yourself.** Refer to your list of "want to's." These can be used as positive reinforcements.

- **Monitor your "screen time."** Students comment frequently on how much time they surprisingly use in front of some sort of screen—TV, computer, video games. These things can be major wastes of time. For example, check your email on a schedule, rather than checking it every half hour. There are also some tools you can use that automatically block certain websites for allotted time periods.

- **Make effective use of your free time.** Rather than "zoning" out in front of the TV, do something relaxing or rejuvenating. For example, listening to music or going for a walk.

- **Avoid procrastination.** Effective ways of doing this include breaking things down into smaller parts. Most often, beginning a task is the hardest part. For example, agreeing to spend at least 20 minutes on an assignment can increase your motivation and willingness to begin. You will often find yourself getting more accomplished than you thought you would.

- **Identify resources and sources of support.** Rather than spending more time than needed on an assignment, make an appointment at the Writing Center or sign up for a Study Skills workshop.

- **Make use of technology.** Outlook, Google and other online platforms allow you to create comprehensive calendars that can include all of your academic, athletic and social responsibilities. In the Resources section of the College Survival Guide, there are additional time management resources that can be utilized.

Reflection Time:
- *What are some things that get in the way of you managing your time more effectively?*
- *What are some things you can do differently in the next week to better manage your time?*

Creating your schedule

When you sit down to create your schedule, be realistic about (a) the amount of time you need per task (b) your attention span, and (c) the free time you will need to allow yourself for a break. While it may initially look like every moment of your life is scheduled, being a successful student-athlete does not mean that there is no time for fun. Part of the time management puzzle is finding ways to work more efficiently and effectively, rather than just "putting in the time." For example, twenty minutes of focused time is more effective than one hour of time with multiple distractions, where you are trying to study for Spanish while checking Facebook and watching your favorite reality show. When creating your daily schedule, you may also want to consider building in time to utilize additional resources such as study skills and writing workshops; these resources are in place to teach you the skills necessary to work smarter, not harder.

Sexual Health

Students enter college with varying degrees of sexual experience. Research suggests that teens are beginning to engage in sexual intercourse at a younger age than they have in the past, so the idea of sexual activity will not be foreign to many college students (NACHIC, 2007). Recent statistics state that about 80% of college students are sexually active (Lambert, Kahn, & Apple, 2003; Paul, McManus, & Hayes, 2000). As a result the greater degree of freedom and independence and the close quarters of campus living, it is important to understand the increased opportunity to make poor or impulsive decisions about sexual relationships. Many of the sexual encounters on college campuses occur within the context of casual sex, or 'hooking up.' Add in alcohol or other substances to these situations and the chances of impulsive behavior, poor decision-making, and costly long-term consequences increases exponentially. While it may be unrealistic to expect that all sexual behaviors students engage in will be done with great deal of care and forethought, there are a number of precautions that students—and especially first-year students—can take that will minimize the risk of making poor, regrettable sexual decisions.

> 49% of upperclass student athletes reported that they rarely or never thought about the negative consequences associated with sexual activity during their first year.

The interplay of substance use and sex can set the stage for a wide array of challenges for college students ranging from STDs to date rape to unwanted pregnancy. Arguably, not one of you reading this text wants an STD, or would choose to raise a child right now. Consequently, it's important to have a plan about how you want to approach your sexual health, which requires you to think about these things *before* you find yourself in compromising situations.

Interpersonal Violence and Hazing

Too often, we hear about interpersonal violence or hazing that has occurred on a college campus. In many circumstances, student-athletes are involved in the ones that make the national news. This is not to say that student-athletes are more likely to engage in these behaviors, but due to the role they play on campuses and the high visibility afforded them, these are the ones we hear about the most. The term "interpersonal violence" is used to suggest any incidence of violence enacted on another person, including rape and sexual assault. On college campuses, this term is used to describe violence occurring between two students, particularly in relationships and more often than not, men against women. However, keep in mind that interpersonal violence occurs in relationships of all types.

Similarly, the act of hazing is often viewed as a rite of passage for first-year students seeking membership into a particular group. Hazing requires individuals to engage in particular humiliating or embarrassing tasks in order to be accepted. To comply with the Title IX regulations, many universities have enacted policies that provide support for students who feel that they have been impacted by issues of interpersonal violence, such as harassment or bullying. Due to their naiveté or lack of experience, first-year students can find themselves in situations where they can become the victims of hazing, or become involved in a situation where interpersonal violence is occurring. Here are some ways to avoid involvement in situations that could end in violence or hazing:

4 Ways to Avoid Interpersonal Violence and Hazing

- **Avoid confrontations when intoxicated.** Emotions typically run high when there are substances involved. Be careful to ensure that you are not having a difficult conversation or confrontation at the wrong time.
- **Find safety in numbers**. Do not put yourself in a compromising situation, or one that you should not be in alone. Make sure that you are not part of a group that contributes to making poor choices.
- **Speak out when you see something wrong.** Bystanders have tremendous power, but unfortunately, many do not come forward because they think someone else will. If you see an inappropriate situation—or completely unfair or just wrong—share it with someone who can take proper action.
- **Surround yourself with good people.** "Birds of a feather flock together" is an old saying based upon the idea that if you surround yourself with good people, those making the best choices, and intervening as bystanders when they see inappropriate actions, it is likely that you will learn from them. Similarly, unfortunate situations seem to follow people who make poor choices.

Managing the Media

Think back over your last year of high school. How many athletes do you remember making headline news as a result of decisions made in front of the media or poor management of social media? One of the most significant changes between the athletes of today and those of even a decade ago is the influx of technology and the fact that there are now multiple forms of media for student-athletes to navigate. In the past and with more traditional forms of media, only one or two athletes were in the public eye, serving as spokespersons for the entire team. Yet, with the developments in technology and the multiple media platforms, every member of an athletic team now has direct media access.

First-year student-athletes must quickly learn that this is yet another way in which college student-athletes and non-athletes differ. For example, while another first-year college student in your Calculus class may be able to get away with tweeting disparaging remarks about her math professor, as a student-athlete, you are held to a higher standard of behavior. Whether that is fair or not is not the point; the bottom line is that student-athletes are much more visible than their non-athlete peers, and even more importantly, they will be seen by many as representatives of the university. In other words, many view your actions as being reflective of the campus name that you wear on your jersey. For this reason, many coaches and teams implement strict policies to minimize the likelihood of your social media decisions becoming front page news. Unfortunately, those policies are not always effective, and since student athletes do not always make such good choices, they often suffer consequences in a way that their peers may not. Here are some ways to avoid the pitfalls that can come as a result of poor management of social media:

---

3 Ways to Manage Social Media

- **Find out what your team policy is around social media and postings.** Following team rules will make it easy to stay out of trouble
- **When in doubt, ask someone else before you press 'send.'** Or better yet, take some time before sending—walk away, think about it, and come back to it before you poorly represent yourself, your team, or your school.
- **If you question whether something is appropriate to post, you should probably NOT post it.**

Reflection Time:
- *Provide three examples of mistakes that college athletes could make utilizing social media.*

Athletic Identity and the Social Transition

As discussed in Chapters 1 and 2, the degree to which you define yourself by your athletic identity can potentially impact multiple areas of your life, not just athletics. The influence of a high athletic identity also impacts your social and cultural transition, both positively and negatively as you navigate your first year. Throughout this chapter, we have discussed in great detail the importance of integrating socially into your campus culture. One way of feeling socially connected is by developing a strong identification with your institution, something that student-athletes often develop simply as a result of wearing your school name and colors on your uniform. Research strongly suggests that this institutional identification, as well as socially integrating into the environment, contributes greatly to retention and overall success as a first-year college student-athlete (Sedlacek & Adams-Gaston, 1992; Tinto, 1987; Woosley & Shepler, 2011).

As a student-athlete, you have a great opportunity for exposure to a wide social network due to the public nature of your role (Horton & Mack, 2000). However, making use of that network is a benefit that student-athletes (especially those with a high athletic identity) must intentionally seek out. Simultaneously, there are also social costs associated with a high athletic identity. For example, individuals may isolate themselves more than others, deciding that the only important relationships to build are those associated with the team and athletic success, or there may be a lack of community and campus involvement, instead focusing solely on sport related connections and pursuits (Miller & Kerr, 2003). As a result, you may make less effort to overcome that barrier and seek to connect—choosing to forgo social interactions with teammates, hallmates, or classmates, deciding instead to watch film, study plays or spend all of your free time working to improve athletically.

One last aspect of a high athletic identity that may potentially impact your social and cultural development is the possibility of limited career exploration (Tyrance, Harris & Post, 2013). Research suggests that college athletes with higher athletic identities tend to have greater expectations to continue to play their sport professionally, and are at risk to make fewer efforts to plan for a non-athletic future or career (Brown, Glastetter-Fender & Shelton, 2000; Riemer, Beal & Schroeder, 2000; Miller & Kerr, 2003; Tyrance, Harris & Post, 2013). Student-athletes may overlook the need to build relationships, engage in networking, or explore career options that are extremely important and can lead to an easier post-athletic career transition. While there is tremendous value to placing a high degree of emphasis on your athletic identity and your growth and development in your sport, you also must ensure a balanced perspective.

Mental Health in the Social/Cultural Transition

There are specific mental health concerns that may develop from the challenges first-year student-athletes experience in navigating the social and cultural transition. Here are some of the more commonly occurring diagnoses that can develop within the context of social interactions, or can be exacerbated by the pressures that first-year student-athletes may experience socially:

Social anxiety: Social anxiety is marked by a fear of being negatively evaluated or judged in a social context (American Psychiatric Association, 2013). Students who struggle with social anxiety sometimes describe themselves as 'shy,' and think that this is the reason they choose not to interact with groups of people or become socially isolated. Similarly, these students may find that they are comfortable interacting with their team-mates—due to the frequent interactions with the same group—but really struggle to connect with students and others within the larger campus. Your first year in college is a time when your social world is expanding, and a part of college success and retention is a result of feeling socially integrated and connected to others.

If you struggle with social anxiety, you may find it extremely difficult to initiate relationships or even follow up with others who offer to build a relationship with you. If you find yourself dreading these interactions, or have difficulties motivating yourself to build relationships with others, you may be experiencing symptoms of social anxiety. In addition, some student-athletes may resort to using substances in order to make these social interactions easier. It is important to keep in mind that there are several resources available to you (teammates, coaches, team sport psychologist, or university Counseling Center), so you do not have to figure out how to manage this challenge on your own.

Depression: Depressive symptoms are frequently marked by low motivation, feelings of sadness, fatigue, isolation, withdrawal, and a lack of enjoyment of previously pleasurable activities (American Psychiatric Association, 2013). Other symptoms of depression can include increased tearfulness, irritability, and difficulty sleeping (or sleeping too much). Athletes who struggle with depressive symptoms often find it difficult to interact with others; they may find themselves having difficulty connecting with teammates or other peers, developing friendships, and becoming increasingly isolated. When students are not aware of the signs or symptoms of depression, they may find it difficult to understand what they are experiencing. Recognizing these symptoms in their earliest form and intervening can decrease the likelihood that they become significantly debilitating.

Eating Disorders: In the social and cultural context, student-athletes may develop or struggle with eating disorders as a result of comparing themselves to the physical appearances of their non-athlete peers. Eating disorders are marked by misperceptions of body image or feelings of low self-worth, often associated with body weight. While eating disorders are more common among females, the rates of these disorders among men are on the rise. Studies suggest that women in particular sports are more at risk for developing these disorders as compared to female non-athletes (Waldron, Stiles-Shipley, & Michaenok, 2001). Sports that emphasize weight restrictions or require revealing uniforms may have higher rates of athletes with eating disorders or disordered eating (O'Connor, Lewis, & Kirschner, 1995; Reel & Gill, 1996; Ziegler, Shoo, Sherr, Nelson, Larson, & Drewnowski, 1998). Beyond eating disorders, athletes may have other issues with body image. For example, first-year female student-athletes who often possess muscular builds or body types that may not fit the campus 'norm,' may find it intimidating to be surrounded by students and in an environment that reinforces a different body type, and therefore may engage in unhealthy eating practices in an effort to alter their body type to fit the social norm.

Substance Use and Abuse: Finally, substance use or abuse is a disorder marked by dependence or inappropriate use of a particular substance—most often nicotine, prescription drugs, alcohol, or marijuana. College campuses in particular are places where students tend to ingest alcohol or marijuana fairly frequently, considering this to be a part of the "college experience" (O'Malley & Johnson, 2002; ACHA, 2009). Additionally, studies indicate that student athletes in general report higher rates of binge drinking than their non-athlete peers (Hildebrand, Johnson, & Bogle, 2001; Leichliter, Meilman, Presley, and Cashin, 1998). Despite the belief that these activities are in some part socially accepted on university campuses, underage drinking and marijuana use (in most states) are both illegal, and result in serious consequences.

The use of any of these substances, even in a small amount, can negatively impact academic and athletic abilities. Additionally, student-athletes are subject to random drug testing, and testing positive for many of these substances can result in suspension or being banned. Another factor to consider in the context of substance use is the possibility of using as a form of "self-medication," or as a "social lubricant." Many people who struggle with undiagnosed social anxiety or depression seek out these substances to make social interactions easier or more enjoyable. If you find that you are depending on a substance to ease social interactions, again, it is time to access the supportive resources available.

International Students and the Social/Cultural Transition

In many ways, international student-athletes may have a greater challenge in navigating the social and cultural transitions as compared to either the academic or athletic adjustment. Depending on your background, you may have limited social support, different exposure and experiences managing the cultural norms of the university, and less knowledge of the environment that would allow you to connect with others and develop meaningful relationships. Despite the presence of an office dedicated specifically to assisting international students in their transition, staff members are not always well versed in the complexities of the world of a student-athlete. For example, one of the difficulties that you may face as an international student-athlete may be a limited opportunity to form relationships with other international students due to scheduling conflicts between student activity programming and athletic practices or competitions.

An additional challenge may be the lack of students from the same area, or those who share the same background, and despite the generic support provided to all international students, the diverse backgrounds could present you with an even greater challenge in integrating with your peers. Yet another obstacle that may occur is the language barrier between teammates, coaches, and other students—both non-athletes and student peers. Language barriers can contribute to anxiety or apprehension around interacting with others. There may be greater hesitance to initiate communication, to ask questions, or build relationships. This lack of social connection and limited access to social support can result in greater isolation, again contributing to less institutional identification, less social integration, and ultimately less overall student success. Considering the challenges that you can face regarding navigating your new environment, here are a few suggestions to connect socially on college campuses:

---

4 Ways for International Student-Athletes to Connect

- **Consider connecting to the off-campus international community and/or organizations**. Most cities or college towns have an international presence that may not be connected with your institution, but can serve as a source of social support. Explore this possibility.

- **Educate your teammates**. Your teammates may not be familiar with various aspects of your cultural background or customs, but may be interested in connecting with you. Be willing to share in ways that may be enjoyable but also help them learn. An example of this may be sharing a meal from your country, or discussing cultural traditions and experiences.

- **Develop relationships with the international student groups.** These groups are important, but don't rely solely on that population. At times, there is a tendency to remain within the group that you feel the most comfortable with, which could limit your ability to build relationships with others, expand your connections and increase opportunities for social support. Make sure you develop relationships with as many groups as possible, including your teammates, non-athletes, and those in the international student organizations, as the members of each group can support you differently.

- **Help recruit other international students**. Helping to bring in other international students may assist you in several ways; it increases your sense of identifying with your institution, helps to increase the diversity of your university, and strengthens your team. Assisting in the recruiting process can also provide other international student-athletes an opportunity and access to higher education, while simultaneously increasing your social network and social support.

Transfer Students and the Social/Cultural Transition

Similar to the athletic adjustments covered in Chapter 2, many of the social and cultural transitions incurred by first-year student-athletes will be experienced by transfer student-athletes. Though being a new student on any campus offers distinctive social challenges, the transfer student experience may be unique due to your previous exposure and possible expectations. One of the benefits of being a first-year student in any environment is that there are often many others sharing in your adjustment. Many first-year students attend meals, social gatherings, and brave the new experiences of college together, helping ease the sometimes painful social transition. Often, first-year student athletes also help each other through exciting new experiences.

Unfortunately, not all transfer students will have the benefit of entering with other transfer students and therefore may have to endure these changes alone. You may be the only transfer student-athlete on your team, and your opportunities to connect with some-one based on a shared experience will be limited. You run the risk of being isolated, in a sort of "no man's land"—between the first-year students on your team who are braving the entire college world for the first time, collectively, and the returning upperclass athletes on your team, having the advantage of previous years together. Additionally, depending on the circumstances that led to your decision to transfer, there may be some "baggage" to navigate, possible negative expectations or comparisons built on those previous experiences that contribute to apprehension or anxiety about creating a new social life.

Some transfer students feel that they struggle to build trust with the rest of their team. In the eyes of their teammates, there may be higher—or at least different—expectations for transfer student-athletes that make it more challenging to connect. For example, transfer students do not enter as the 'blank slates' that many first-year student-athletes do; they are either expected to be much more prepared, and therefore much less ready to step in and contribute or conversely seen as late-bloomers needing the guidance of more advanced student-athletes. Your teammates may view you as an unknown entity, may see you as greater competition, and may have increased apprehension around bringing you into the social group as a result of that concern. Along with the possible greater expectations that coaches and teammates may have of you, there may also be greater internal pressure that you place on yourself to come in and make an impact quickly. This may result in you being more closed off from others, or contribute to an egocentric and solely athletic focus, potentially leading to a decrease in motivation and less focus on building those relationships. In some cases, as a transfer student, you may be coming into a team that you have played against in the past, contributing to additional barriers in developing relationships. Again, these are challenges that first-year student-athletes do not typically have to navigate.

Other factors that can play a role in managing the social and cultural transition for transfer student-athletes is the change in university or city environment, the university climate toward student-athletes, or the arena in which social interactions occur. Students transferring from large universities to smaller schools may feel that they have fewer options for social connection than they once did; vice versa, students transitioning from smaller schools to bigger institutions may feel overwhelmed by the larger environment with more people and less opportunity for building more meaningful relationships.

The shift required in the adjustment from one environment to another can be a challenge. Transfer students who have attended universities in more "college friendly" towns have mentioned finding it difficult to transition into an urban environment where the university campus is not necessarily the center of the community social scene. Similarly, students have expressed difficulties trying to build social relationships when the social scene occurs on campus, which may require a personal connection and invitation. Another contributing factor that transfer students may find as a barrier is the campus climate and public perceptions of student-athletes. For example, on campuses where student-athletes may be viewed with more 'celebrity status,' they are afforded greater social access and connections. Student-athletes who transfer from such a university to a campus that places less value on athletics, or even has negative perceptions of student-athletes, may experience additional difficulties navigating that social transition. Keeping each of these factors in mind, here are some suggestions to help transfer student-athletes navigate the social life at a new institution.

6 Ways for Transfers to Manage the Social Adjustment

- **Be patient**. Change and adjustment takes time. It takes time to learn your new environment. Prove yourself and build trust. Try not to rush it, and try not to panic.

- **Concentrate on your team relationships first**. It may be tempting to build relationships outside of the team first, and move toward team relationships as they occur. Instead, focus on building those team bonds, especially since they will often be the most challenging to make, but can yield the greatest benefits, both on and off of the court.

- **Try not to make comparisons**. Comparing every experience in your new environment to the experiences at your former institution can set you up for tremendous failure. You don't want to live in the past because it will make it almost impossible to move forward. Work hard to remain focused on your current environment and live in the present.

- **Take advantage of having a "clean slate."** You have an opportunity to build new relationships the way you would want to have them develop. We do not often have a chance to start over. You may benefit from seeing this new experience as an opportunity to do just that.

- **Do your research.** Make sure you learn about the social life and opportunities that your new institution will have available to you; similarly, make sure you are aware of the possible changes you may have to make in terms of school and community climate.

- **Keep an open mind**. Do your research. It's hard to completely know what to expect from any new experience. Different does not always mean bad—exposure to many new situations, people, and experiences, is often a good thing.

Discussion Questions

1. What are some signs that diversity is valued on your campus?

2. What are areas of diversity that you find to be most challenging or uncomfortable? Why?

3. What are three things you can do to use your time more efficiently over the next two weeks?

4. What are two ways to avoid making poor choices around sexual health?

5. What are two ways to avoid making poor choices around interpersonal violence?

Journal Space

_____

_____

_____

_____

_____

_____

Part II: The College Survival Guide

Segment I: Self-Awareness

Segment II: Academic Success

Segment III: Social Adjustment & Life Skills

Winning at the College Level

INTRODUCTION

Winning at the College Level is a practical guide to navigating your first-year in college, preparing you for the experiences that will accompany your transition into the world of college athletics, and providing you with tools to skillfully manage the adjustment. Consistent with Part I, the College Survival Guide workbook gives you the resources to assess your values as a student-athlete, skills to increase your academic success, and the awareness to optimize your social experiences. The activities in this guide are structured to encourage self-reflection while simultaneously helping you develop concrete strategies that can be implemented on a daily basis to enhance your overall college experience.

The first section of the College Survival Guide is structured around the central theme of recognizing, understanding, and organizing your personal values. We begin with a values checklist, which allows you to identify your most important values (athletic, academic, and social). Understanding the principles you consider to be most important plays a foundational role in how you view yourself, set your goals, and manage your time. Therefore, after selecting your values, you are asked to assess your athletic identity – the level to which you identify with the athletic role. After determining your level of athletic identity, we include worksheets that allow you to set goals in each of the three areas. Regardless of the strength of your athletic identity, it is imperative that you establish and work towards goals in the academic and social arenas. Finally, the values section closes with information and practical tools that will help you develop essential time management skills, successfully manage your time requirements, gain an understanding of what is important to you (values and identity), set appropriate goals and wisely working towards achieve them.

The second segment of the College Survival Guide focuses on increasing your opportunity for academic success. One way to expand your understanding of who you are as a student is to gain insight into your preferred learning style. You are given an opportunity to reflect on your learning preference, and provided tips and study strategies associated with each learning type. Once you gain a better understanding of your preferences, you will be more equipped to tackle the two primary forms of assessment and evaluation for most college classes—test taking and writing. The test preparation section provides guidance on note taking (reading and lecture), study skills and taking exams. Similarly, the writing skills section provides a framework for developing and organizing writing assignments.

The final segment of the workbook emphasizes techniques and provides tools to enhance your social adjustment – commonly identified as life skills. This section includes information and activities on communication styles, decision making, stress management and financial management. Having a framework for your communication style and understanding how others communicate with you is an asset in building all types of relationships (with coaches, teammates, roommates, and professors). Due to the large number of new experiences that college offers, good decision making is critical. This guide outlines a decision making model to help you analyze the way in which you make decisions, and offers you a process for approaching important choices.

A component of decision making is emotional intelligence/EQ. EQ provides a structure for understanding yourself and others. A key component of EQ is self-regulation and impulse control, and being able to recognize the situations that trigger strong emotional responses can increase your ability to make better decisions, even in the midst of difficult positions. Finally, the last two areas that we explore are stress and financial management. Building a strong foundation in both of these areas is critical to your overall happiness. Stress is a natural element of any transition, and obtaining coping skills early in your college career will build your tolerance and increase your potential for success. In addition, financial difficulties can lead to stress and poor decision making; therefore, tools have been included to help build your financial literacy. In summary, while this section is geared towards your social adjustment, the development of these skills can add to your academic and athletic success and are essential to building quality relationships in college and beyond.

This College Survival Guide is designed to give you guidance and tools to help you build the skills necessary to have a successful first-year. You will get the most out of the workbook by thoroughly completing the activities, and consistently putting the strategies into practice. You have the tools…it is your responsibility to take control of your college career. Have a GREAT first-year!

Segment I: Self-Awareness

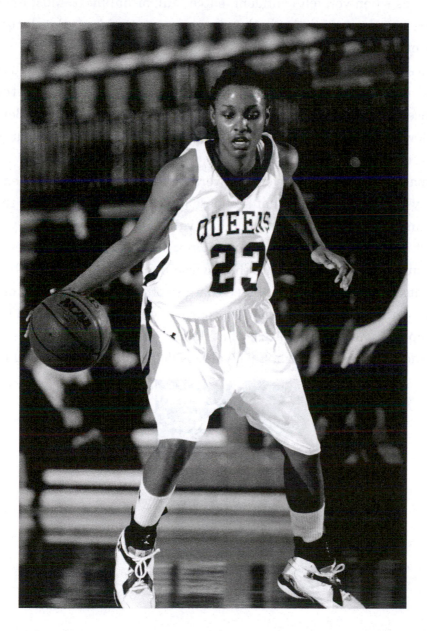

Winning at the College Level

Section 1: Understanding Your Values

Do you know what your values are? What are the four or five things that are most important to you? Think about these questions in terms of your own principles or morals; what are those things that need to be present in order for you to feel that you can be successful, or enjoy yourself? If you think back to your experiences in high school—athletic, academic, or social—you will recognize that there is a consistent pattern present during those times when you felt confident, successful, or happiest. Most likely, if you can identify the common characteristics in those experiences, you have developed an understanding of your values.

This workbook begins with values because they are foundational. Your values influence and drive your motivations, behaviors and decision-making, and they can provide guidance as you navigate the new experience of college athletics. Being aware of your values allows you a more clear lens through which you can create your goals and work towards accomplishing them.

While many of your values overlap several domains—athletic, academic, and social—you may have some values that are more important in one domain than in the others. For example, you may place tremendous value on structure within your academic domain, but not at all in your social domain. Again, being able to recognize what is most important to you will help you to create the environment that you need to be successful.

On the next page 39 terms are listed that are often used to identify or describe values related to athletics, career, school, or your personal life. Go through the list and identify your top five values in the areas of athletics, academics, and your social life, and place them in the appropriate boxes. Each value is defined on the following pages.

Worksheet 1.1: VALUES CHECKLIST

From this list of values, identify your top five in each category and place them in the chart below. If there are some terms that come to mind that are not listed, please add them to the list in the blank spaces.

Variety	Achievement	Creativity
Autonomy	Challenge	Sense of community
Competition	Cultural Diversity	Excitement
Recognition/Fame	Independence	Friendships
Fun	Helping others	Influence
Impact society	Knowledge	Learning
Personal development	Legacy	Balance
Power	Loyalty	Stability/Security
Risk	Teamwork	Adventure
Efficiency	Excellence	Relationships
Reputation	Responsibility	Self-Respect
Time Freedom/Flexibility	Wealth	Leadership
Intensity	Aesthetics	Affiliation
_____	_____	_____
_____	_____	_____

ATHLETIC VALUES	ACADEMIC VALUES	SOCIAL VALUES
1.	1.	1.
2.	2.	2.
3.	3.	3.
4.	4.	4.
5.	5.	5.

Values: Definition of Terms

Variety: enjoying different types of activities and having an appreciation for new and different things; flexibility

Achievement: feeling a sense of mastery or sense of accomplishment

Autonomy: ability to work alone or independently, with little oversight or management; a need for freedom in work

Creativity: ability and appreciation for tasks requiring imagination or innovation; something allowing for the development of new ideas; artistic expression

Challenge: the desire to push yourself and stretch in order to learn and grow; enjoying the sense of accomplishment received from achieving difficult tasks

Sense of community: the need to feel connected and integrated into a larger group of people

Competition: striving to be the best within a group; enjoying being put against others

Cultural Diversity: being surrounded by people from various backgrounds, cultures, experiences, and beliefs

Excitement: drama, fast-pace, sense of adventure, high stimulation

Recognition/Fame: receiving public accolades and credit for efforts and achievements; having others admire and look up to you

Independence: flexibility and freedom; being able to have some control over the direction and details of what you do

Friendships: developing good relationships with others through working together that may be able to expand to multiple areas

Fun: freedom to be playful and enjoy yourself; entertaining

Helping others: assisting or serving people directly, either individuals or groups

Influence: having the ability or opportunity to change or shape decisions, people, or organizations

Impact society: contributing to the growth and development of the larger community or world

Knowledge: ability to learn, understand, and develop, either by experience or observation

Learning: continual acquisition of knowledge

Personal development: opportunity to be self-reflective and integrate experiences to allow for growth

Legacy: being able to leave a mark for others to remember you by

Balance: being able to provide the appropriate amount of energy to multiple areas

Power: the ability to control or influence the behaviors of others or being able to impact the outcome of important events

Loyalty: being able to commit or provide unwavering support to an institution or environment; feeling a sense of institutional or environmental support

Stability/Security: consistency and predictability; an environment or situation that is likely to remain the same

Risk: sense of challenge or danger; the presence of potential for high success or failure

Teamwork: opportunities for collaboration or the need to work with others to accomplish a goal

Efficiency: maximizing outcome with limited wasted effort or energy

Excellence: consistently creating high quality outcomes

Relationships: placing high value on interactions between individuals; wanting to be deeply connected to other people

Reputation: placing high value on how others view you and the work you do

Responsibility: opportunities to be in charge or have control over the outcome of a situation or task

Self-Respect: being able to behave in a way that is consistent with your values

Time Freedom/Flexibility: having the ability to manage your time as you feel is the most effective

Wealth: having the potential to accumulate monetary rewards or financial gain

Leadership: Guiding a group of people or a project; having the opportunity to impact or influence individuals, whether in a formal or informal manner

Intensity: an environment that allows for a great deal of emotion and effort

Aesthetic: the presence of a sense of beauty or an appreciation or concern with the attractiveness of the physical surrounding

Affiliation: having a strong sense of belonging, connection, or identification with a group of people or institution

Section 2: Assessing Your Athletic Identity

As we mention in the chapter on Athletic Transitions, most athletes who get the opportunity to compete at the collegiate level tend to view themselves through an athletic lens. Research suggests there are both costs and benefits to having a high athletic identity, and at the extreme end there may be a greater priority for growth and development in the athletic arena with the exclusion of academic or social development. Your level of athletic identity has the potential to dictate the values you identify with as well as the decisions you make.

Take five minutes to complete the Athletic Identity Measurement Scale (AIMS) included below. This scale is used to evaluate how much an individual identifies with the athletic role, with higher scores on this scale indicating a higher athletic identity (Brewer & Cornelius, 2001). Total scores range from 7-49; the average score for male college student-athletes is 39, and the average score for female college student-athletes is 38. A higher than average athletic identity could make you vulnerable to unhealthy practices in and out of sport, while a lower athletic identity may make it difficult to engage in the necessary actions needed to achieve athletic success.

Worksheet 2.1: ATHLETIC IDENTITY MEASUREMENT SCALE

For each statement below, please circle the number that best reflects the degree to which you agree or disagree with each statement in relation to your own sports participation. Total your score for each of the seven questions to find your level of athletic identity.

Statement	Strongly Disagree						Strongly Agree
1. I consider myself an athlete.	1	2	3	4	5	6	7
2. I have many goals related to sport.	1	2	3	4	5	6	7
3. Most of my friends are athletes.	1	2	3	4	5	6	7
4. Sport is the most important part of my life.	1	2	3	4	5	6	7
5. I spend more time thinking about sport than anything else.	1	2	3	4	5	6	7
6. I feel bad about myself when I do poorly in sport.	1	2	3	4	5	6	7
7. I would be very depressed if I were injured and could not compete in sport.	1	2	3	4	5	6	7

Reprinted with permission from Britton Brewer, Ph.D.

Worksheet 2.2: EXPLORING YOUR ATHLETIC IDENTITY

- What is your total score? _____

- Is your score above or below average? _____

- How does that impact the decisions you make or your behaviors?

  _____

  _____

  _____

- Review your completed values checklist. How does your score on the AIMS impact your athletic, academic, and social values?

  _____

  _____

Section 3: The Importance of Goal Setting

In Chapter 2, we compared goals to a road map- they give you a sense of direction and purpose, and allow you to understand where you are heading. Without a map, it is easy to drift along with no sense of guidance or structure; similarly, without goals it is easy to move about aimlessly. Now that you have clarified your values, you can use those to help you establish goals for yourself in each of the domains you have been exploring: academics, athletics, and social.

As we explained in Chapter 2, a well-written goal is more likely to be effective, and there is a particular way in which a "good" goal should be created. There are several types of goals: long term, short term, subjective, process, performance, and outcome. For the purposes of this workbook, we want to focus primarily on process and outcome goals.

Most often when we set goals, they are typically outcome goals, or goals that are focused on a result. Wanting to become an All-American in track and field or the desire to achieve a certain grade on an exam would both be examples of outcome oriented goals. While it's good to establish goals that focus on the end result, you also need to establish process goals. Process goals focus on the steps that you would need to take in order to make that outcome goal more likely. For example, setting the process goals of studying for at least twenty minutes a day, meeting with a tutor once a week, and getting at least seven hours of sleep the night before the exam are all steps that would increase the likelihood of getting an A on the exam—if that was your outcome goal.

Again, referring back to goal setting in Chapter 2, we echo the research suggesting that goals need to be SMART: Specific, Measurable, Attainable, Realistic, and Time bound (Smith, 1994). Each of the process goals described to achieve an A on that exam fit these criteria:

- Study at least twenty minutes a day.
- Meet with the tutor once a week.
- Get at least seven hours of sleep the night before the exam.

The next three worksheets give you the opportunity to set goals in the three areas we have been focusing on throughout this text. Using the values you determined to be most important on the values checklist (Worksheet 1.1), establish three outcome goals and the coinciding process goals—i.e., the steps you would need to accomplish along the way to make achieving those goals more likely. Your outcome goals can be short-term, something you want to achieve this month or semester, or longer term, focused on the academic year or your overall college experience.

Worksheet 3.1: ATHLETIC GOAL SETTING

OUTCOME GOAL 1:

      Process Goal 1:

      Process Goal 2:

      Process Goal 3:

OUTCOME GOAL 2:

      Process Goal 1:

      Process Goal 2:

      Process Goal 3:

OUTCOME GOAL 3:

      Process Goal 1:

      Process Goal 2:

      Process Goal 3:

*Specific*___

*Measurable*___

*Attainable*____

*Realistic*____

*Timely*____

Worksheet 3.2: ACADEMIC GOAL SETTING

OUTCOME GOAL 1:

      Process Goal 1:

      Process Goal 2:

      Process Goal 3:

OUTCOME GOAL 2:

      Process Goal 1:

      Process Goal 2:

      Process Goal 3:

OUTCOME GOAL 3:

      Process Goal 1:

      Process Goal 2:

      Process Goal 3:

*Specific*____

*Measurable*____

*Attainable*____

*Realistic*____

*Timely*____

Worksheet 3.3: SOCIAL GOAL SETTING

OUTCOME GOAL 1:

     Process Goal 1:

     Process Goal 2:

     Process Goal 3:

OUTCOME GOAL 2:

     Process Goal 1:

     Process Goal 2:

     Process Goal 3:

OUTCOME GOAL 3:

     Process Goal 1:

     Process Goal 2:

     Process Goal 3:

Specific____

Measurable____

Attainable____

Realistic____

Timely____

Section 4: Time Management

The ability to manage your time effectively will contribute to your successful navigation of the academic, athletic, and social transitions you will encounter throughout your college career. As a student-athlete, much of your time is accounted for, with limited unstructured time. While first-year students who are not athletes are faced with the demand of balancing the academic and social worlds of college, you have another world to balance that requires a great deal of time and energy.

Effective time management is a necessary skill that can be developed, and we have provided you with a framework to begin honing that skill. As a first-year student-athlete, you have a limited amount of available free time, and utilizing that time in the most productive manner can be the difference between merely surviving during your first year and thriving. Successful time management requires that you keep track of and complete all of your mandatory activities, while also integrating and engaging in activities that can serve as stress relievers. You will also need to be mindful of patterns that may serve to increase your non-productive time. We provide you with three worksheets that can be used for each semester of your first year.

The first worksheet offers you an "at-a-glance" view of your semester schedule, which allows you to keep track of all of your upcoming athletic travels, exams, and university breaks. An example is provided that you can use as a template and is based on the spring semester at one university. You can use a method of tracking that works best for you: for example, different colored texts may be an easy way to differentiate between home and away games. This system lets you see potential scheduling conflicts in advance, increases your ability to be prepared, and decreases the negative impact that can result from having to balance multiple time demands.

The second worksheet offers you a daily schedule where you can write out all of your time obligations. We suggest you fill in the times for class, practice, study hall, treatments, and competitions. In addition to those mandatory activities, insert times for sleeping and meals—especially breakfast and lunch, since they will provide you with fuel for practice. Also include times to study on your own, as well as time for social activities. It is important to be realistic in the way you build your schedule since your ability to create and adhere to a comprehensive schedule will increase your likelihood of success in the athletic, academic, and social realms of your college experience.

The third worksheet is a log that allows you to examine your free time in a very clear format. You can track the number of hours a week that you spend in required activities—practice, classes, study hall, sleeping, etc—quantify the hours you have left over, and consider the most effective division of that time in order to meet your academic, athletic, and social requirements. There are only 168 hours in a week, and a certain number of those hours are accounted for with mandatory activities. This includes sleep, as at least 7-8 hours a night is recommended. Without awareness of the time you have remaining, you run the risk of wasting time, becoming overscheduled, and failing to manage necessary tasks.

Finally, because we know that time can easily slip by you, the last worksheet allows you to keep track of the non-productive ways you may be tempted to use your time. We call these "time wasters," or activities you engage in that do not serve a productive purpose but are also not 'relaxing' in the sense of being strategically scheduled and used to recharge your internal battery or give yourself a break. They are simply activities that you may use to escape or allow yourself to procrastinate (i.e. video games, constantly updating your status on social media, or "zoning" out in front of the television), therefore eating into your productive time. These time wasters can possibly contribute to even more stress in the long term when you fail to complete your tasks. Don't forget that technology can be helpful in allowing you to manage your time effectively. Make use of apps or computer programs that might make this task easier.

SEMESTER AT-A-GLANCE (EXAMPLE)

Sunday	Monday	Tuesday	Wednesday	Thursday	Friday	Saturday
Jan 12	13	14	15	16	17	18
19	20 **Holiday**	21	22 ECON Problem Set	23	24	25
26	27	28	29 Away Game	30	31 SOC Paper	Feb 1
2	3	4	5	6	7 ECON EXAM	8
9 Home Game	10	11 ECON Problem Set	12	13 CHEM EXAM	14	15 Home Game
16	17	18 PSYCH EXAM	19	20	21	22
23	24	25	26	27 Home Game	28 ECON EXAM	March 1
2	3 **Spring Break**	4 **Spring Break**	5 **Spring Break**	6 **Spring Break**	7 **Spring Break**	8
9	10	11	12	13	14	15
16	17 Away Game	18	19 PSYCH Lab	20	21 ECON EXAM Home Game	22
23	24	25	26	27 Conference Meet	28 Conference Meet	29 Conference Meet
30	31	April 1 SOC Paper	2	3	4 PSYCH EXAM	5
6	7	8	9	10	11	12
13	14	15	16 SOC EXAM	17	18 **Holiday**	19
April 20	21 **Holiday**	22	23	24	25 ECON EXAM	26
27	28	29 SOC Paper	30	May 1	2 **FINALS**	3 **FINALS**
4	5 **FINALS**	6 **FINALS**	7 **FINALS**	8 **FINALS**	9 **FINALS**	10 **FINALS**
11	12	13	14	15	16	17

Worksheet 4.1: FIRST SEMESTER AT-A-GLANCE

Sunday	Monday	Tuesday	Wednesday	Thursday	Friday	Saturday

Created by and used with permission from Wendy LeBlanc, Senior Academic Learning Specialist at Tulane University.

Worksheet 4.2: FIRST SEMESTER DAILY SCHEDULE

Using the following schedule, plan out the details of your day. Include time for sleeping, attending classes and practice, studying, and meals. Also include 'free time' or some time for you to relax during the day. Make every effort to be realistic in your evaluation of your schedule; for example, if you know you have a difficult time studying directly after practice, it may be helpful to schedule this time as 'free time.'

	Monday	Tuesday	Wednesday	Thursday	Friday	Saturday	Sunday
8:00 am							
9:00am							
10:00am							
11:00am							
12:00pm							
1:00pm							
2:00pm							
3:00pm							
4:00pm							
5:00pm							
6:00pm							
7:00pm							
8:00pm							
9:00pm							
10:00pm							
11:00pm-8:00am							

Worksheet 4.3: FIRST SEMESTER TIME REQUIREMENTS

Time management is about using the time that you have available in the most efficient way possible. In order to manage your time effectively, you must first make an assessment of your time. There are a total of 168 hours in a week. What are the mandatory time requirements in your schedule? This would include class time, study hall, practice time, competition time, and time for sleep.

Activity	Total Hours per Week
Class	_____
Mandatory study hall	_____
Practice	_____
Competition	_____
Sleep	_____
Number of hours/week	**168**
	--
YOUR TOTAL HOURS of MANDATORY ACTIVITY	_____
Time available for additional activities	_____

Keep in mind that your additional activities need to include activities essential to your academic, athletic, and physical success (i.e., eating, studying, and relaxation time). List five of your additional activities in the spaces below. For example, if you work, attend additional tutoring sessions, church or other religious services, or volunteer on a consistent basis, include each activity, along with an estimation of the number of hours a week you spend engaged in that activity.

Activity	Total Hours per Week
_____	_____
_____	_____
_____	_____
_____	_____
_____	_____

Worksheet 4.4: SECOND SEMESTER AT-A-GLANCE

Sunday	Monday	Tuesday	Wednesday	Thursday	Friday	Saturday

Created by and used with permission from Wendy LeBlanc, Senior Academic Learning Specialist at Tulane University.

Worksheet 4.5: SECOND SEMESTER DAILY SCHEDULE

Using the following schedule, plan out the details of your day. Include time for sleeping, attending classes and practice, studying, and meals. Also include 'free time' or some time for you to relax during the day. Make every effort to be realistic in your evaluation of your schedule; for example, if you know you have a difficult time studying directly after practice, it may be helpful to schedule this time as 'free time.'

	Monday	Tuesday	Wednesday	Thursday	Friday	Saturday	Sunday
8:00 am							
9:00am							
10:00am							
11:00am							
12:00pm							
1:00pm							
2:00pm							
3:00pm							
4:00pm							
5:00pm							
6:00pm							
7:00pm							
8:00pm							
9:00pm							
10:00pm							
11:00pm-8:00am							

Worksheet 4.6: SECOND SEMESTER TIME REQUIREMENTS

Time management is about using the time that you have available in the most efficient way possible. In order to manage your time effectively, you must first make an assessment of your time. There are a total of 168 hours in a week. What are the mandatory time requirements in your schedule? This would include class time, study hall, practice time, competition time, and time for sleep.

Activity	Total Hours per Week
Class	_____
Mandatory study hall	_____
Practice	_____
Competition	_____
Sleep	_____
Number of hours/week	**168**
	--
YOUR TOTAL HOURS of MANDATORY ACTIVITY	_____
Time available for additional activities	_____

Keep in mind that your additional activities need to include activities essential to your academic, athletic, and physical success (i.e., eating, studying, and relaxation time). List five of your additional activities in the spaces below. For example, if you work, attend additional tutoring sessions, church or other religious services, or volunteer on a consistent basis, include each activity, along with an estimation of the number of hours a week you spend engaged in that activity.

Activity	Total Hours per Week
_____	_____
_____	_____
_____	_____
_____	_____
_____	_____

Worksheet 4.7: TRACKING YOUR "TIME WASTERS"

In order to use your time most effectively, it is necessary to limit your engagement in unproductive behaviors. While it is important to schedule free time for fun and relaxation, it is crucial that you are mindful of those behaviors that do not provide you with any tangible benefit. Identifying and tracking time wasters will allow you to reduce or eliminate these activities, increasing your ability to remain on task and accomplish your goals. Below are activities commonly identified as distractions for college students; we have included two extra spaces to add distractions that are not listed. Spend one week tracking the amount of time spent engaging in these activities.

Activity	Hours per day	Total hours per week
Social media	_____	_____
Video games	_____	_____
Unhealthy relationships	_____	_____
Email communication	_____	_____
Texting/cell phones	_____	_____
Watching TV/movies	_____	_____
Partying	_____	_____
Surfing the web	_____	_____
_____	_____	_____
_____	_____	_____

Segment II:
Academic Success

Winning at the College Level

Section 5: Learning Style Preferences

Self-awareness is a key to success in any endeavor, particularly when you are transitioning into a new experience. Your understanding of your preferred style of learning increases the likelihood for success in both the academic and athletic areas of your new college experience. There are many models that explore learning styles, but for the purposes of this text, we use a relatively simple framework to build your understanding.

Fleming and Mills' (1992) model of learning styles, categorizes learning preferences into four primary types: visual, auditory, reading, and kinesthetic. We concentrate on only three: visual, auditory, and kinesthetic, as these are the three most commonly used (Barbe & Swassing, 1988). The first learning style sheet (Worksheet 5.1) presents you with 10 reflection questions to help you gain insight into your potential learning style preference. The worksheets that follow provide more information on key characteristics for each learning style preference, as well as study tips to enhance understanding and retention, and increase learning success.

If you find yourself interested in gathering more information about your learning style preference and how it influences your performance in the classroom and on the field, we encourage you to follow up with your Academic Support Center. They will be able to provide you with guidance, suggestions, resources, and possibly even a formal assessment to evaluate your learning profile.

Worksheet 5.1: WHAT IS YOUR PREFERRED STYLE?

In order to do a thorough assessment of your true learning style, a comprehensive psychoeducational evaluation would be required. However, with a few questions, you can gather valuable knowledge around how you take in information, store it, and access it to lead to greater academic success.

V = Visual Preference   A = Auditory Preference   K = Kinesthetic Preference

Questions to consider:
1. How do you prefer to study?
    V: By reading the textbook or looking at diagrams.
    A: By reviewing what I've learned and explaining it to someone else.
    K: By taking notes or drawing diagrams.

2. If your coach explains something to you, you are likely to remember it best if:
    V: They show me a diagram, and draw it out for me.
    A: My coach explains it to me.
    K: I draw it out for myself, or I physically run through the steps.

3. When traveling, do you prefer to:
    V: Use a map or GPS.
    A: Ask for directions.
    K: Start driving and figure it out as you go.

4. If you have free time, you prefer to:
    V: Watch a movie or read a book.
    A: Listen to music or an audio book.
    K: Do something that is "hands on", like building a model car.

5. Which of the following courses would you enjoy most:
    V: One that requires a great deal of reading (i.e., English or Literature class)
    A: One that depends on learning more from listening to the professor lecture
    K: One that requires a great deal of learning by doing (i.e., chemistry or engineering)

6. When it comes to enjoying sports, you would prefer to:
    V: Read about it or watch it.
    A: Hear about it or listen to it on the radio.
    K: Simply play.

7. What type of board game would you prefer to play with friends?
      V: Scrabble or Words with Friends.
      A: Charades.
      K: Twister or Jenga.

8. When you cook, you would prefer to prepare a new dish by:
      V: Following the recipe by reading it.
      A: Calling someone and having them tell me how to make it.
      K: Begin to make it and figure it out along the way.

9. You prefer a teacher who conducts class by:
      V: Using PowerPoint slides or other types of slides while they teach.
      A: Relying on lectures, explaining information with little or no visual input.
      K: Requiring a great deal of interaction or classroom activities.

10. When you have to make a major decision or solve a problem, you would prefer to:
      V: Write, using diagrams or making a list of pros or cons.
      A: Talk things out with others or to myself.
      K: "Run through it" or engage in physical activity to help me think.

After reading through the list of questions and considering what you know about yourself, you may find one style resonates more with you than the other two. The remaining pages in this section will provide you with pointers to help you better understand each of the styles, navigate your classroom experiences, and develop study habits that will increase the possibility of academic success.

Totals:

V: _____

A: _____

K: _____

Worksheet 5.2: VISUAL STYLE PREFERENCE

Students who express a preference for accessing and retaining information presented in a visual manner tend to prefer reading as their primary mode of obtaining information. They may have a tendency to take notes to retain information and find that they close their eyes when provided instructions, in an effort to visualize the content. Students who prefer this style may enjoy watching things in order to learn, and the use of diagrams or illustrations may be vital to increased understanding of concepts.

Key characteristics of those with visual style preference:

- You need to see what you are learning, to understand it more fully.

- You prefer presentations or illustrations, graphs, and charts to spoken discussion.

- You may become easily distracted by competing oral or auditory stimuli.

- If directions are presented orally, you may find yourself looking at others to understand what you should do.

- You may zone out when information is presented in a lecture format only.

Here are some pointers to help those who identify more with a visual style:

- Draw things out or create a diagram or flowchart to aid in your understanding and retention of information.

- When you study, create illustrations or put words into pictures to help you grasp concepts.

- Create flashcards, which require you to copy over notes to help you remember information.

- Print out the PowerPoint slides before class, leaving spaces to write additional notes during lectures.

- Make use of highlighters or underlining as you read the text to pull out important information.

- During exams, recall the pictures or diagrams you created to answer questions.

Worksheet 5.3: AUDITORY STYLE PREFERENCE

Students who express a preference for accessing or receiving information using an auditory style often rely on orally presented information. They may have the tendency to read aloud to themselves as they study, or teach others in the process of acquiring knowledge. Visually presented information or competing auditory cues may serve as distractions.

Key characteristics of auditory style preference:
- You may sit where you can hear the lecture, but you don't necessarily need to see the instructor or the board in order to remember.

- You might close your eyes to attend to information or focus, rather than be distracted by competing visual stimuli.

- You would prefer to attend class, rather than rely on the PowerPoint slides posted to understand course content.

- You may try to spell words by sounding them out rather than writing them down.

Here are some pointers to help those who identify more with an auditory style:
- Repeat information out loud or verbally review with teachers or peers to gain a greater understanding of information.

- Attend and lead study groups, which will allow you to teach others.

- Record lecture classes.

- Create a story integrating information or using specific examples to increase retention of study material, or put information you are attempting to learn in a rhythmic pattern.

- During exams, think about how you would explain your answers to someone else before writing them down.

Worksheet 5.4: KINESTHETIC STYLE PREFERENCE

Students who possess a strong preference for accessing information in a kinesthetic manner tend to learn best by touch and movement. You may find that you enjoy more lab based classes, or opportunities to engage in more hands-on learning. If this is your preference, you may retain information more easily if you move around while studying, or take frequent breaks.

Key characteristics of kinesthetic style preference:

- You tend to express yourself with your hands, or rely on touch to enhance learning.

- You take abstract concepts and try to make them more concrete.

- You might prefer learning through use of trial and error rather than reading or being told what to do.

- You may find movement and activity by others more distracting than visual or auditory distractions.

Here are some pointers for those who tend to have a kinesthetic style preference:

- Try studying or reading while using an exercise bike, treadmill, or while engaging in other physical activity.

- In the course of an exam, recall knowledge gained from field trips or lab activities to spark your memory.

- Use role-play or act out scenarios to help commit information to memory.

- Make connections between course content and real life examples.

- Complete practice tests or examples on a chalkboard or white board while studying.

- Find a non-distracting way to move your body (i.e. Doodle, chew gum, take notes, squeeze a stress ball) while listening to orally presented information to enhance retention.

Section 6: Test Preparation

Most often, the primary goal of study sessions, taking notes, and attending class is to prepare you for exams. In many college courses, the majority of your grade depends on your performance on mid-term and final exams. As a result, you will be best prepared by completing each of these tasks with a specific purpose: test preparation. The worksheets in this section will provide you with key points to remember as you navigate the academic demands of your college courses and offers templates to help organize relevant course content.

In the college classroom, the ability to take effective notes is a skill that can be the key difference between simply completing and excelling. Students that can take notes well are more successful in identifying key themes and the relevant information as they listen to lectures or read texts. They are then at an advantage, particularly if they get into the habit of reviewing their lecture notes or text notes on a relatively consistent basis. These students are more equipped when it comes to exam time; rather than spending the night before cramming or having to re-read the chapter, they can use their time more efficiently by reviewing quality notes.

We have provided you with two templates that offer options for taking notes while listening to a lecture or taking notes while reading. Though the style of note taking outlined may be of greatest benefit to those who identify primarily with a preference for information presented visually, every student—across all learning style preferences—can benefit from the structure provided. *(Note Taking strategies are listed on pages 140-141)*

Once you have learned how take notes more effectively, it is equally important to learn to leverage your notes to strengthen your study skill set. Many students enter college with the belief that their study skills are well developed; after all, without them, you may not have gotten to college! However, many first-year college students often realize that they did not really need to study hard in high school, and the higher academic rigor of college courses results in the need to strengthen this skill set. Fortunately, most campuses have an Academic Support Center and possibly an Athletic Academic Support Center that provides workshops on study skills; we encourage you to make an appointment early in your academic year and begin building these skills as quickly as possible. We have outlined some of the most effective study tips for you to integrate into your test preparation strategies. *(Study Skills strategies worksheet page 152-153)*

Ultimately, the reason to hone your skills on note taking and study skills is to increase your effectiveness in taking tests and examinations. Test taking is also impacted by your ability to write effectively and concisely (writing skills will be discussed in more depth in Section 7). Your test taking approach should differ based on the type of exam you are preparing for and completing. The tips you will find most effective will differ for essay exams, multiple choice exams, or examinations that are a combination of the two. In the section on test taking , we outline tips specific to essay and multiple choice tests. *(Test Taking strategies page 154-155)*

NOTE TAKING

Taking, editing, and reviewing notes are some of the most important skills to understanding course content and increasing knowledge. We provide two worksheets that can serve as templates for note taking—both in the classroom and while reading. However, it is not enough to simply take good notes—your notes must also be reviewed within 24 hours, which will allow you to edit or revise them for maximum clarity and retention. We have created and included a structure that you can take to each of your classes that will help you to organize lecture notes and other important information covered in class.

The first worksheet is a template for taking notes during class or lecture. There is a space provided for the date, the class or course (i.e., Psychology 101) and the lecture topic (i.e., Personality). Follow the format of the template and jot down the key concepts introduced during the lecture (i.e., structure of personality, grand theories of personality, assessing personality). The text box at the top of the page is a good place to jot down key themes as they are presented. Most professors will either write out key concepts on the board or display them on a PowerPoint slide (or other visual media); these are themes that will be helpful to include in your text box. As you make note of these key themes, understand that you do not need to capture every word mentioned, but make sure you use examples to illustrate your points when possible. Also keep in mind that the posted Power-Point slides are usually just a portion of the content that is covered on tests, and you should not rely solely on these as study guides.

There is also a section of the template that allows you to write down questions that come up during the lecture that you may want to ask your professor about later, or explore for yourself in the textbook. If you do not have time after class to ask your professors questions, don't be afraid to ask your question in your next class, send an email, or make use of your professor's posted office hours. Be sure to add the clarification they provide to your notes. Your notes are most effective when you review them after a lecture, filling in the spaces with more specific information that can guide you as you study. Here is where you may want to make use of the textbook or posted PowerPoint slides to further enhance your notes and better prepare you for exam questions based on the lecture.

The second worksheet serves as a template for note taking as you complete the required (or suggested) reading for a course. You will want to begin with a quick overview—you can skim the text for this information—of the reading to identify learning objectives or key concepts that the author wants you to understand. Additionally, with that overview, think about your professor, his or her teaching style, and the course objectives that may have been outlined on your syllabus. This information will provide greater clarity for discerning important information and indicate where you should spend more of your attention and focus.

Most course textbooks outline the chapter learning objectives at either the chapter's beginning or end, and there is a place on the worksheet that allows you to jot down those objectives. As you move through your readings and gather information about each objective, you will want to highlight key terms, data, and ideas that will provide further illustration of the concepts. As you outline the relevant evidence for each objective, make sure you put the information in your own words, or apply it to examples provided in class. This will reinforce your learning and reduce your need to re-read your textboxes (in detail) as you prepare for exams or tests. Taking the time to complete the note taking worksheets while you read will provide you with ready-made study guides. These worksheets, in combination with your note sheets from lectures are a great start to successfully manage any course.

Worksheet 6.1 – NOTE TAKING TEMPLATE #1

Date: _____   Class: _____

Lecture Topic: _____

```
┌─────────────────────────────────────────────────────────────────┐
│  Key Themes of the Lecture:                                       │
│                                                                   │
│                                                                   │
│                                                                   │
└─────────────────────────────────────────────────────────────────┘
```

Major Concept _____   Major Concept _____

_____   _____

Supporting Facts   Supporting Facts

-   -

-   -

-   -

-   -

-   -

-   -

FOLLOW UP QUESTIONS: **FOLLOW UP QUESTIONS:**

_____   _____

_____   _____

_____   _____

_____   _____

_____   _____

Worksheet 6.1 – NOTE TAKING TEMPLATE #2

Date: _____   Class:_____

Lecture Topic: _____

Key Themes of the Lecture:

Major Concept _____   Major Concept _____

_____   _____

Supporting Facts   Supporting Facts

-   -

-   -

-   -

-   -

-   -

-   -

FOLLOW UP QUESTIONS: **FOLLOW UP QUESTIONS:**

_____   _____

_____   _____

_____   _____

_____   _____

_____   _____

Worksheet 6.1 – NOTE TAKING TEMPLATE #3

Date: _____   Class:_____

Lecture Topic: _____

Key Themes of the Lecture:

Major Concept _____   Major Concept _____

_____   _____

Supporting Facts   Supporting Facts

-     -

-     -

-     -

-     -

-     -

-     -

FOLLOW UP QUESTIONS: **FOLLOW UP QUESTIONS:**

_____   _____

_____   _____

_____   _____

_____   _____

_____   _____

Worksheet 6.1 – NOTE TAKING TEMPLATE #4

Date: _____   Class:_____

Lecture Topic: _____

Key Themes of the Lecture:

Major Concept _____   Major Concept _____

_____   _____

Supporting Facts   Supporting Facts

-   -

-   -

-   -

-   -

-   -

-   -

FOLLOW UP QUESTIONS: **FOLLOW UP QUESTIONS:**

_____   _____

_____   _____

_____   _____

_____   _____

_____   _____

Worksheet 6.1 – NOTE TAKING TEMPLATE #5

Date: _____   Class:_____

Lecture Topic: _____

Key Themes of the Lecture:

Major Concept _____   Major Concept _____

_____   _____

Supporting Facts   Supporting Facts

-   -

-   -

-   -

-   -

-   -

-   -

FOLLOW UP QUESTIONS: **FOLLOW UP QUESTIONS:**

_____   _____

_____   _____

_____   _____

_____   _____

_____   _____

Worksheet 6.2: NOTE TAKING TEMPLATE #1

Date: _____   Reading Topic: _____

Learning Objectives:
-
-
-
-

Objective 1:

_____

_____

Relevant Evidence (in your own words)

_____

_____

_____

Objective 2:

_____

_____

Relevant Evidence (in your own words)

_____

_____

_____

Objective 3:

_____

_____

Relevant Evidence (in your own words)

_____

_____

_____

Objective 4:

_____

_____

Relevant Evidence (in your own words)

_____

_____

_____

Worksheet 6.2: NOTE TAKING TEMPLATE #2

Date: _____   Reading Topic: _____

Learning Objectives:
-
-
-
-

Objective 1:

_____

_____

Relevant Evidence (in your own words)

_____

_____

_____

_____

Objective 3:

_____

_____

Relevant Evidence (in your own words)

_____

_____

_____

_____

Objective 2:

_____

_____

Relevant Evidence (in your own words)

_____

_____

_____

_____

Objective 4:

_____

_____

Relevant Evidence (in your own words)

_____

_____

_____

_____

Worksheet 6.2: NOTE TAKING TEMPLATE #3

Date: _____   Reading Topic: _____

Learning Objectives:
-
-
-
-

Objective 1:

_____

_____

Relevant Evidence (in your own words)

_____

_____

_____

Objective 3:

_____

_____

Relevant Evidence (in your own words)

_____

_____

_____

Objective 2:

_____

_____

Relevant Evidence (in your own words)

_____

_____

_____

Objective 4:

_____

_____

Relevant Evidence (in your own words)

_____

_____

_____

Worksheet 6.2: NOTE TAKING TEMPLATE #4

Date: _____   Reading Topic: _____

Learning Objectives:
-
-
-
-

Objective 1:

_____

_____

Relevant Evidence (in your own words)

_____

_____

_____

_____

Objective 3:

_____

_____

Relevant Evidence (in your own words)

_____

_____

_____

_____

Objective 2:

_____

_____

Relevant Evidence (in your own words)

_____

_____

_____

_____

Objective 4:

_____

_____

Relevant Evidence (in your own words)

_____

_____

_____

_____

Worksheet 6.2: NOTE TAKING TEMPLATE #5

Date: _____   Reading Topic: _____

Learning Objectives:
-
-
-
-

Objective 1:

_____

_____

Relevant Evidence (in your own words)

_____

_____

_____

Objective 2:

_____

_____

Relevant Evidence (in your own words)

_____

_____

_____

Objective 3:

_____

_____

Relevant Evidence (in your own words)

_____

_____

_____

Objective 4:

_____

_____

Relevant Evidence (in your own words)

_____

_____

_____

STUDY SKILLS TIPSHEET

We have already mentioned the need to review and revise your notes within 24 hours of taking them, adding clarifying information and including examples and additional explanations as needed. There are a few additional tips and strategies we would recommend to increase the likelihood of studying effectively and retaining important information for academic success. Here are some tried and true methods of getting the most out of your study time:

- **Don't try to multitask**. Despite the common belief that some people benefit from 'multitasking', research shows your performance on each task suffers when you attempt to complete more than one task at a time. If you are going to study, do just that—study. Turn off the SportsCenter updates, close out of Facebook and Google chat, and study!

- **Break your time into "bite sized" chunks**. If you know that your attention span is relatively limited, you will be better served by giving yourself shorter periods of study time on a more consistent basis. For example, study uninterrupted for about 30 minutes, give yourself a five minute break, and hit the books again for another 30 minute session. Similar to building muscles through weight training, you can gradually increase your tolerance and your attention span by building on this foundation.

- **Study consistently**. A 20 to 30 minute daily study session for each subject is more effective and is likely to yield more positive results than a five-hour study session the night before an exam.

- **Connect your concepts to real world examples**. Rote memorization efforts may have paid off in high school, but this strategy will have limited effectiveness in a college course, where the learning objectives are achieved through critical thinking. If you are able to connect course concepts to situations you can understand in "real life," you will be more prepared to respond to assessment questions that are application based or require critical thinking.

- **Take advantage of your mandatory study hall sessions**. If you are at an institution that requires first-year and transfer student-athletes to attend study hall, use the time as effectively as possible. Seek out extra help from tutors, review your class notes from the lectures of the day, or read the assigned text for the week. Rather than using this time effectively, many student-athletes are resentful and may squander the hours socializing or being consumed by social media. As a result, they end up having to use their "free time" to accomplish these important tasks.

- **Find a consistent method of studying that works best for you**. Attend classes prepared, and use the note taking template to guide you in that process. The better prepared you are, the better notes you will take, and the more effective you will be in studying. Adapt the note taking strategies to your preferred learning style; for example, if drawing an outline or a concept map is more aligned with your learning style, integrate that approach into your note taking. In addition, use the information from your preparation and performance on your first exam to help alter your study methods for future exams.

- **Teach someone else**. One of the best ways to ensure that you have a firm grasp of a concept is to try to explain it to someone else. This is one of the benefits of building relationships with other members of your class, regardless of their athletic status. Studying in groups and explaining the idea or concept to someone else in your own words is a great measure of how well you've learned the information.

TEST TAKING TIPSHEET

Make no mistake, being able to take tests well is a skill, and one that can be strengthened, the same as any other skill. While tests are designed to evaluate the amount of learning that has occurred in a class, they are also designed to assess attention, study skills, and critical thinking. Here are a few general strategies to enhance your test performance, regardless of the type of test you are taking:

- **Get a good night sleep the night before your exam, and eat a good breakfast**. Even if you cram, sleep is essential for learning and solidifying all of that last minute exam preparation. Additionally, the glucose provided from eating before your exam can actually enhance your memory, recall, and focus during your exam.

- **Arrive early for exams.** Plan to arrive at least ten minutes before your exam is scheduled to begin. When you are rushing to arrive on time, anxiety levels increase in an already stressful situation, which can contribute to test anxiety. Arriving early allows you to find the "perfect" seat, locate the restrooms (keeping in mind that your exam may not be in the same room as your classes) and helps you to be 'clear-headed' and ready to respond to any question you are presented with.

- **Scan the entire exam first, including the directions and the point allocation for each section**. In order to make the most effective use of your time, it is important to know how the exam is laid out. If the first questions are multiple choice and the last few are short answer but are worth more than the multiple choice questions, it may be more effective to spend your time focused on the questions that count the most first.

- **Read each test question carefully**. Most students read the first few words of a test question, and assume they know what information it is asking for. Take the time to read each word in the question. Some test questions may be tricky in what they ask for (i.e. which response is the LEAST accurate, or which response does NOT meet the criteria). Additionally, some questions may ask you to respond to more than one question, and you may lose points for failing to respond to each question asked.

- **Relax, and trust your preparation**. Similar to the confidence that comes from your athletic preparation, take confidence in your academic preparation. If you have done the work needed, you should feel prepared to do well on any exam; relax, and let the work you have done show in your performance. Many students suffer from test anxiety and blank out or freeze during exams, which prevents them from demonstrating their knowledge. However, if you are able to prepare well and trust in that preparation, this anxiety is unnecessary.

- **Review your responses before turning in your exam.** Reviewing your responses will help you to realize if you have misread a question, or approached it from an incorrect perspective.

- **Bring the required materials with you to the exam.** Depending on the class and the professor, this might include: calculator, scantron, blue book, etc.

Completing Multiple Choice Questions

- **Read the entire question first.** Underline the "key words" in the question.

- **Come up with a response to the question.** Use your own words before looking at the choices.

- **Eliminate the choices that you know are incorrect.** You can usually "rule out" at least two of the four choices, which are typically the most extreme.

- **Be careful of choices that include the terms "always" or "never."** These are easily refutable.

Completing Essay Questions

- **Analyze the question, underlining or numbering the multiple questions or parts involved.** Jot down the key ideas you are familiar with, and outline your response based on those concepts. Make sure you provide a response to each and every question or part. If you only respond to three of the four questions, you will only receive 75 percent credit—at most.

- **Set a time limit for each question.** If you have four or five questions to answer (and if they all share the same point value) evenly divide your time to ensure that you do not find yourself with twenty minutes left and three questions unanswered.

- **Only include information that you 'know' for certain.** Do not feel obligated to elongate a response or add fluff to increase your word count or fill space. This expansion of a vague response can result in the inclusion of incorrect information and a loss of points.

- **If you run out of time, quickly write down everything you know.** Most professors grade essay exams or short answer questions by applying partial credit. If you quickly include the information that you know, even without the benefit of connections or complete sentences, it could be enough to display your general understanding of the concept.

Section 7: Writing Skills

Writing skills are important to your success as a college student. Unfortunately, many high schools do not teach the requisite skills necessary to become an effective college-level writer. Most universities are equipped with a Writing Center as a part of their formal academic support services, so we suggest that you take full advantage of these resources as early as possible. The writing process in its simplest form has five phases: brainstorming, outlining, drafting, proofreading/revising and finalizing. We have included some important tips for you to refer to during the process of completing your writing assignments, as well as a worksheet we suggest you use as a template to help construct an outline for your writing assignments. The worksheet is a brief outline of the important components of most well written papers, and the following describes each area of the worksheet:

Topic: This is your main idea, theme, or purpose of your paper. Most writing assignments are clear about the purpose and specific content. The topic sentence should serve as a central point of reference, and all of the content should connect somehow to this topic. Your opening or introductory paragraph should clearly outline your topic, provide a broad overview of your ideas, and include your thesis statement.

Thesis statement: Your thesis statement is usually comprised of one sentence that lets the reader know what your perspective is as the writer. This statement informs the reader of the concepts introduced throughout the body of the paper; it can sometimes take the form of an opinion and introduce the sources you plan to use to support that opinion.

Supporting Details: Your thesis statement should be confirmed by at least five supporting details, which serve as a rationale for your argument. Each supporting detail should be expanded into at least one paragraph to expound upon your initial idea.

Summary/Conclusion: The conclusion of your paper should include a reference to your initial topic or thesis statement, as well as a brief statement summarizing the support you have presented in the body of your paper.

Key Concepts: This section of the worksheet is included to allow you space to jot down the information requested in your writing assignment. Including this information on your writing worksheet allows you a point of reference for all key concepts and ideas that must be included to completely respond to the requirements of your writing assignment.

Worksheet 7.1: WRITING ASSIGNMENT TEMPLATE

Writing Topic: _____

Thesis Statement: _____

_____

_____

Supporting Details:

1.

- _____

- _____

2.

- _____

- _____

3.

- _____

- _____

4.

- _____

- _____

5.

- _____

- _____

KEY CONCEPTS TO INCLUDE:

Summary/Conclusion:

_____

_____

_____

_____

WRITING SKILLS TIPSHEET

Writing is hard work; so do not be discouraged if it's an area you struggle with. You can get better by practicing, revising, and rewriting. To write properly, you must write complete sentences, using correct grammar and punctuation. Your professors and future employers may even correlate your aptitude and intelligence with your writing abilities, so it is a skill you should work on as much as you can throughout college. Writing papers requires adherence to standard rules of grammar, spelling, and punctuation—do not use abbreviations, misspellings, or lack of punctuation as you might while you are texting or communicating with friends electronically. When writing for your professors, remember that formal writing requires you pay careful attention to the basic rules of grammar and style, since mistakes have a way of overshadowing the content of your writing. Ask yourself before turning in a paper or other writing assignment if you have been clear, coherent, and complete.

Below are common errors to avoid in your writing. Consult your Writing Center for more in-depth writing support. Don't forget to run spell check before turning in your writing assignments, but don't rely on it to fix everything for you.

- **A sentence needs a subject and a verb.** Ex.: *He runs. She rows. They won.*

- **Sentence fragments are not sentences. A sentence fragment cannot stand on its own because it does not have both a subject and a verb.** Ex.: *Since she left here; started the race; yesterday when I ran a mile.*

- **A run-on sentence, also called a fused sentence, is essentially a sentence that is not punctuated correctly, where two or more independent clauses are joined without a conjunction.** Ex.: *I am a goalie I am a freshman.*

- **Use conjunctions—*and, but, or*—to fix run-on sentences.** Ex.: *I am a goalie, and I am a freshman.*

- **Use punctuation to correct run-on sentences, but be careful to use it correctly.** Ex.: *I am a goalie. I am a freshman* is correct; however, *I am a goalie, I am a freshmen* is not correct because the comma incorrectly splices together two complete sentences, and that's not the comma's job.

- **It is the period's job to separate complete sentences. A semi-colon joins two independent clauses (i.e., clauses that could stand alone as a complete** sentence) to show a close relationship or a bond between statements. Ex.: *I won the lifting challenge; Coach gave me a day off.*

- **Commas have many uses, and like other punctuation, exist to make order of writing on the page.** The ways commas can be used include: between items in a series; to attach words to the front or back of your sentence; and to join two sentences with a conjunction. Ex.: *We will read, study, eat, and practice today. Certainly, it will take a lot of focus. Tomorrow we are going to practice penalty shots, and today we are watching game tapes.*

- **Don't use "big" or complex words to impress professors if there are simple words that get your message across.** Often students try to gain formality in their writing by inserting words from a thesaurus without understanding the meaning. These words can alienate or confuse readers. Aim for your writing to flow well.

- **Be on the look-out for common errors that even spell check cannot detect**, such as the difference between your/you're; it's/its; then/than; whether/weather; lose/loose; affect/effect; which/that; farther/further; lay/lie.

- **Read your work aloud before turning it in.** This helps you recognize issues with both grammar and content. It also helps you recognize repetition of phrases or content.

- **Revise and rewrite your work often. If you start your assignments early, you are in a better position to ask for help.** Ask your professor, teaching assistant, writing tutor, or friend to read a draft in advance of your deadline to see if you're on the right track and how you can improve.

- **There are many other rules of punctuation and grammar, and the best way to improve your writing is to ask others for critical review of your writing.**

Created by and used with permission from Sara Gebhardt, Ph.D. – Professional Writing Consultant and Adjunct Professorial Lecturer, American University.

Segment III:
Social Adjustment
&
Life Skills

Winning at the College Level

Section 8: Communication Styles

Effective communication is essential for building and maintaining all forms of relationships. This includes your relationships with teammates, coaches, roommates, friends, and significant others. One hallmark of developing healthy relationships is having some awareness of your predominate style of communication. Prior to entering college, most student-athletes have been surrounded by the same teammates and coaches for many years and have adapted to the dynamics of those particular relationships. However, college presents a host of new relationships to navigate, and having a general framework of major styles of communication can help you as you begin to forge those relationships.

As referenced in the relevant section of Chapter 3, there are four predominate communication styles: *passive, assertive, aggressive and passive-aggressive.* Depending on the particular situation as well as the type of relationship, most of us are able to use each of these styles. However, there is typically a style that we rely on most often and resort to particularly in situations of high emotion or conflict. Developing an awareness of the style you most often use allows you to appropriately apply your style when the situation calls for it. Understanding each communication style also allows you to share information in a way that others are more likely to receive it. Awareness of your style and the styles of those around you is a difficult transition to make as you manage new relationships, but having an awareness of these styles will allow you to develop better relationships more quickly with those around you. This is very important as you only have four or five years to form healthy college relationships!

Worksheet 8.1: <u>ASSESSING YOUR COMMUNICATION PATTERNS</u>

The following information will help you to determine your predominate style of communication. Use the questions presented below to help you clarify your patterns of communicating with others, keeping in mind that your style will often vary depending on the situation or the relationship.

P = Passive   A = Aggressive   PA = Passive Aggressive   S = Assertive

Scenarios to consider:

1. **In situations of conflict, you are more likely to:**
   P: Avoid the situation and/or remain silent.
   A: Try to impose your will or power over others, or control the situation.
   PA: Use sarcasm or verbalize agreement but behave contrarily.
   S: Directly approach the conflict with respect while clearly expressing your needs in a calm and forthright manner.

2. **When mistakes occur, you are more likely to:**
   P: Keep quiet, even if it means taking the blame for something that you did not do.
   A: Demand the responsible party be identified and even reprimanded.
   PA: Downplay the impact of the error, but harbor resentment or anger internally.
   S: Acknowledge the mistake and begin to work with others to find a solution.

3. **When you are upset about something or with someone, you are more likely to:**
   P: Keep those emotions to yourself, or blame yourself for the situation.
   A: Demonstrate your anger by yelling, threatening, or demanding.
   PA: Deny your anger but behave in a manner that displays your unhappiness (i.e., deciding not to speak to someone; slamming doors; taking your emotions out on someone else).
   S: Find an appropriate time to respectfully express your emotions and consider the other's perspective.

4. **When you meet someone new, you are more likely to:**
   P: Greet them with a limp handshake, demonstrating limited eye contact.
   A: Greet them with an overly firm handshake and strong eye contact, maybe stepping into their personal space to establish dominance.
   PA: Greet them using body language or facial expressions that are inconsistent with your emotional state (i.e., excited and overly exuberant, despite feeling differently).
   S: Greet them with a firm handshake, good eye contact, making a genuine attempt to connect with the person.

5. **In a situation of compromise or negotiation, you are more likely to:**
   P: Give into the other person or the other side without taking into consideration your own needs.
   A: Demand that others give into your needs using force or other means of intimidation, if necessary.
   PA: Initially verbalize happiness with the compromise or decision but display body language or behaviors that indicate displeasure.
   S: State your goal clearly, but work to create a win-win situation where both sides benefit.

6. **If someone asks you to do something you do not want to do, or is against your values, you are more likely to:**
   P: Keep your opinion to yourself, and just go along with them and do what is asked.
   A: Aggressively demonstrate your displeasure and refuse.
   PA: Say yes, but feel resentful and used, or fail to come through at the last minute.
   S: Say no, and explain the situation or value that has contributed to your decision.

7. **If someone gives you negative feedback or constructive criticism, you are more likely to:**
   P: Readily agree, placing all blame on yourself and personalizing the criticism.
   A: Respond with anger and refuse to reflect on the quality or accuracy of the feedback.
   PA: Respond apologetically or in agreement, but harbor feelings of resentment and a desire to retaliate.
   S: Reflect on the value and accuracy of the feedback, and attempt to integrate the feedback into future behaviors.

Totals:

P: _____

A: _____

PA: _____

S: _____

Section 9: Decision-Making and Emotional Intelligence

Effective decision-making is essential to success in the classroom, on the court, and in every other area of life. An individual's decisions are impacted by factors too numerous to list; however, a person's level of emotional intelligence, including impulse control, plays a major role in the choices that they make. In order to successfully navigate the first-year, you must be strategic and thoughtful in your decisions. First-year students are bombarded daily with challenging decisions that can have a major impact on academic, athletic, and social success. These decisions can range from when to study, what to eat for dinner, how to use your free time, or responding to peer pressure around substance use. Each of these decisions has potentially negative (and positive) consequences, and to manage each of the choices effectively, you should have a consistent process of analyzing the advantages and disadvantages of each option.

In this section, we provide information to help increase your awareness of your decision-making tendencies and give you the tools to make healthy and informed decisions. The decision-making model below provides you with a framework to examine the strengths and weaknesses of the choices you are faced with, and to evaluate the outcomes of your decisions. One contributing factor to your decision-making process is your level of emotional intelligence. Emotional Intelligence consists of five components: self-awareness, self-regulation, social skills, empathy, and motivation. There are several different methods often used to assess Emotional Intelligence in individuals, and a detailed assessment is beyond the scope of this text. However, developing the self-awareness to identify your skill set in each of these areas gives you a foundation from which you can leverage your strengths and develop in your areas of weakness. Lastly, most people are enticed to make poor decisions by a set of personal physical or emotional triggers. The following worksheets will allow you to evaluate your decisions, reflect on your Emotional Intelligence, and identify your triggers to impulsive behaviors. Completing an honest evaluation of where you stand in these areas will increase the likelihood of making better decisions and transitioning smoothly throughout your first year of college.

Worksheet 9.1: DECISION-MAKING MODEL

Use the following framework to examine the next moderate-to-major decision you face.

Step 1: Identify the decision (i.e., should I attend a party this evening or stay in the dorm and prepare for an exam later in the week?).

Step 2: List all possible options.

Step 3: Outline the advantages and disadvantages of all options involved.

Step 4: Make an *informed* decision.

Step 5: Evaluate the outcome of your decision.

Worksheet 9.2: ASSESS YOUR EMOTIONAL INTELLIGENCE

Self-Awareness: this term defines how well you know yourself. This would include the knowledge of your strengths and weaknesses, an understanding of dangers and pitfalls that could contribute to failure, as well as an awareness of your emotional response in any given situation and among other people.

- Is my assessment of my strengths and weaknesses consistent with the external feedback I have received from others—coaches, teammates, friends, teachers? Provide evidence to support your response.

  _____
  _____
  _____

- How well do I assess the moods of others, and am I aware of how my mood and displayed emotions impact those around me—friends, family, teammates? Provide evidence to support your response.

  _____
  _____
  _____

Self-Regulation: this term defines your ability to take in information and process before jumping to conclusions or taking action. A descriptive term that may be more familiar or more frequently used is impulse control—the ability to control your emotions rather than allow your emotions to control you. Individuals who are able to self-regulate can delay instant gratification with the understanding that it may result in greater long-term gain.

- In times of high emotion, how well am I able to acknowledge how I feel and choose not to act on those emotions until there is an appropriate time and in an appropriate manner? Provide a specific example to support your response.

  _____
  _____
  _____

- How consistently am I able to analyze all options, possibilities, and consequences prior to making a decision or taking action (i.e., spending money, planning trips, engaging in sexual activity, consuming alcohol or other substances)?

_____

_____

_____

Social Skills: this term defines your skill set in developing interpersonal relationships and managing social situations. One is adept in this area by having the capacity to effectively create networks, build personal and professional relationships, and increase the social comfort of those with whom you interact. Strength in this area increases the chance for success both on and off the field.

- How well do you adapt to social situations, even when you may not know any other individuals around you? Provide evidence to support your response.

_____

_____

_____

- How confident are you in your ability to make friends or build meaningful relationships with your teammates or people outside of your team? Provide evidence to support your response.

_____

_____

_____

Empathy: this term is defined by your ability to understand and put yourself in the "emotional shoes" of others, to get a sense of how they may be feeling. This skill allows you to discern what others may need in a particular moment, and treat them accordingly.

- How effective are you at identifying the emotions and feelings of others and providing them the assistance or support they may need in the moment? Provide an example that speaks specifically to your ability in this area.

_____

_____

_____

- How conscious are you in consistently acting in a way that takes into account the mood or emotional state of others around you? Provide a specific example to support your response.

  _____

  _____

  _____

Intrinsic Motivation: this term defines the internal drive that allows you to take action, accomplish goals, and strive to attain personal fulfillment. Motivation can be the result of internal forces, where actions and desires are completed for the sake of personal enjoyment or for its own sake, intrinsic motives. By comparison, extrinsic motivation comes from external forces, where the rewards and praise resulting from a behavior influences future actions. Being intrinsically motivated allows you to persist even when confronted with disappointment or adversity. Individuals with higher levels of emotional intelligence tend to be driven by more intrinsic factors (self-improvement, self-fulfillment, etc.) than extrinsic rewards (money, fame, praise, etc).

- How well do you persist in pursuing your goals when obstacles or barriers present themselves? Provide an example to support your response.

  _____

  _____

  _____

- What are the factors that lead you to work toward pursing long term goals, challenging yourself, and continuous improvement?

  _____

  _____

  _____

Worksheet 9.3: TRIGGERS TO IMPULSIVE BEHAVIORS

Identifying the specific triggers that may contribute to impulsive behaviors can help you to make healthy choices when these situations occur, rather than succumbing to the automatic behaviors that you may have engaged in in the past. Circle those experiences or situations that can serve as triggers for impulsive or problematic behaviors. There are also additional spaces to add triggers that have not been included.

Lack of sleep	Hunger	Receiving criticism
Disappointment	Making a mistake	Winning a competition
Losing a competition	Relationship difficulties	Substance use
Physical illness	Injury	Loneliness
Bored	Frustration	Feeling disrespected
Teammate conflict	Roommate challenges	Failing an exam
Anger	Sadness or depression	Stress
Fear or being threatened	Financial difficulties	Anxiety or discomfort
_____	_____	_____

Now that you have identified some of your triggers that can lead to impulsive behaviors, list at least six healthy alternatives for managing these situations when they occur (ex.: take a walk; talk to a friend):

_____   _____

_____   _____

_____   _____

Section 10: Stress Management

Throughout this text we have discussed the multiple challenges associated with the transition into college for student-athletes. As with any major change or transition, there is a great deal of stress, which must be carefully managed to limit the potential negative impact that may be experienced. In many ways, the term "stress" has a negative connotation; however, we forget that it actually serves a function. There are two forms of stress: eustress, which is the stress that is associated with positive events—for example, leaving home to attend college or getting married—and distress, which is associated with negative events. Whether the event is positive or negative, our response to stress is a function of our perception of the event and our belief in the capacity we have to manage that event. If we believe that we are equipped to manage the stressors we face, our stress response is pretty minimal; however, if we feel we have a limited ability to deal with the situation, our response can be more dramatic and have a greater negative impact.

We all have an optimal level of stress—too much is overwhelming and can lead to depression and anxiety, and too little leaves us unmotivated to act or accomplish goals. In order to develop effective stress management techniques, we have to learn to identify those things that cause us stress, develop an awareness of how we respond to stressors, and create a game plan that we can put into action to manage the situation. The following worksheets will allow you to identify the multiple ways that individuals can respond to stress (physically, emotionally, cognitively, and behaviorally) and identify which symptoms are particular to you. They also provide information on some of the most effective methods of managing stress to help you develop optimal mental and physical health.

Worksheet 10.1: ASSESS YOUR STRESS SYMPTOMS

Stress can take the form of cognitive, physical, emotional, and behavioral symptoms. Using the chart below, identify the top five symptoms that you recognize in yourself when you are stressed. There are additional spaces where you can add any symptoms that are not listed.

Emotional Symptoms	Cognitive Symptoms	Behavioral Symptoms	Physical Symptoms
Increased irritability	Indecisiveness	Isolation	Lethargy and fatigue
Lack of motivation	Difficulty concentrating	Procrastination	Headaches, back pain, and body aches
Feelings of failure	Racing thoughts	Use of substances to cope	Diarrhea or constipation
Decreased satisfaction and enjoyment	Forgetfulness or memory challenges	Anger directed towards others	Increased or decreased appetite
Increased anxiety	Poor decisions	Crying spells	Frequently sick
Feelings of loneliness	Poor productivity	Grinding teeth	Elevated heart rate and blood pressure
Feeling overwhelmed	Boredom	Eating more or less	Trembling
	Pessimism	Sleeping too much or too little	Nausea

_____

_____

_____

_____

_____

Worksheet 10.2: EFFECTIVE STRESS MANAGEMENT STRATEGIES

There is often a set of strategies we depend on to re-energize us when we experience too much stress. Interestingly, we are not always aware that they are actually management strategies when we implement them—they may just be things we do automatically or have always done. Below is a list of effective stress management strategies that you can add to your current toolbox. Identify at least five management strategies to implement in the next few weeks.

Healthy eating	Get a good night of sleep	Take mini-breaks	Exercise
Establish healthy relationships	Develop a support network	Learn to say 'no'	Communicate effectively with others
Laugh or use humor	Progressive muscle relaxation	Yoga	Challenge your negative thoughts
Change your attitude or perspective	Clarify your personal values	Engage in spiritual practices, including meditation or prayer	Engage in nurturing activities, such as taking a bath
Manage your time effectively	Write things down	Don't procrastinate: do it NOW	Ask for help
Plan ahead	Talk it out	Do one thing at a time	Limit caffeine intake
Get to know your professors	Hug someone	Organize	Take some time every day to do one thing you enjoy

_____

_____

_____

_____

Worksheet 10.3 - JOURNALING

Some writing exercises help with more than just becoming a proficient writer. The act of keeping a journal can lead you toward positive personal growth. The ancient tradition of journaling, or keeping a diary, increases your understanding of yourself and the world around you. The act of regularly writing down your thoughts, frustrations, and successes has been proven to allow people to:

- Decompress from a stressful workload/schedule
- Make better decisions and solve problems
- Arrive at clarity regarding thoughts, feelings, and dilemmas
- Improve physical well-being by dealing with mental stressors

Writing routinely will provide insight on what makes you happy and successful, and what drains you or threatens your emotional well-being. The key to deriving these benefits is to carve out a regular time each day to write freely for five to ten minutes. It's easy. Write in stream of consciousness, meaning you need not focus on correcting your grammar or word choice. You just need to write down your thoughts and feelings without censoring or editing them, and see where the page takes you.

You can use a pen and paper or electronically set up a blog or document that only you can access. The key to journaling is maintaining the privacy of your thoughts. You may decide to look back on your entries in the future to gauge your growth and patterns of behavior, or it's also okay to throw away your entries at any point, since the benefits occur while you are penning your thoughts.

For five to ten minutes, take time out of your day each morning when you wake up or each night before you go to bed. Use the space below to start your first journal entries. So, go ahead, and write freely about whatever comes to mind. Or you can use some of the below prompts to get you started.

- Did you have a disagreement with your coach, a professor, or your teammates? Write about how you feel about it.
- Have you been logging record stats in your sport?
- What makes you confident and happy?
- What is it like to be a first-year student-athlete?
- What makes you angry or sad?
- What is one wish you'd like to be granted in the next week, month, or year?

Journal Entry #1

_____

_____

_____

_____

_____

_____

_____

_____

_____

_____

_____

_____

_____

_____

_____

_____

_____

_____

_____

Created by and used with permission from Sara Gebhardt, Ph.D. – Professional Writing Consultant and Adjunct Professorial Lecturer, American University

Journal Entry #2

_____

_____

_____

_____

_____

_____

_____

_____

_____

_____

_____

_____

_____

_____

_____

_____

_____

_____

_____

_____

_____

_____

Created by and used with permission from Sara Gebhardt, Ph.D. – Professional Writing Consultant and Adjunct Professorial Lecturer, American University

Journal Entry #3

_____
_____
_____
_____
_____
_____
_____
_____
_____
_____
_____
_____
_____
_____
_____
_____
_____
_____
_____

Created by and used with permission from Sara Gebhardt, Ph.D. – Professional Writing Consultant and Adjunct Professorial Lecturer, American University

Journal Entry #4

_____

_____

_____

_____

_____

_____

_____

_____

_____

_____

_____

_____

_____

_____

_____

_____

_____

_____

_____

_____

_____

_____

_____

_____

_____

Created by and used with permission from Sara Gebhardt, Ph.D. – Professional Writing Consultant and Adjunct Professorial Lecturer, American University

Journal Entry #5

_____

_____

_____

_____

_____

_____

_____

_____

_____

_____

_____

_____

_____

_____

_____

_____

_____

_____

_____

Created by and used with permission from Sara Gebhardt, Ph.D. – Professional Writing Consultant and Adjunct Professorial Lecturer, American University

Section 11: Introduction to Financial Management

You may wonder why we chose to include a worksheet on financial management in this text. An additional aspect of the freedom that comes with attending college is an increase in financial freedom and responsibility. Most students no longer have someone standing over them to observe the way they spend their money or to manage it for them. Couple that freedom with the ability to sign up for credit cards and purchase items that are nonessential or may even be discouraged at home, and this can lead to early financial troubles that may have long term negative impacts on your financial future. In addition, your decisions around spending and managing your finances are potentially connected to your ability to self-regulate and manage your impulses to spend money with little planning or long term thought.

The following worksheet will offer you some brief tips on the do's and don'ts of navigating the financial aspects of your first year of college. We also include worksheets that will allow you to create a budget and track your weekly spending to help you recognize your purchasing patterns and identify poor spending habits. Some students may have received these lessons in high school; however, the freedom that exists within the college context can offer a unique challenge and change your ability to effectively apply those lessons.

FINANCIAL
MANAGEMENT TIPSHEET

- **Do** create a budget and stick to it!
- **Do** start a checking account at a local bank, or one near your university.
- **Do** buy used or rent books when possible.
- **Do** pay all of your bills on time. This includes your cable bill, your cell phone bill, and your utilities. Managing these first bills well can help you begin to establish a positive credit history.
- **Do** think long term before making major purchases. It is recommended that you wait at least 30 days before making a major, nonessential purchase.
- **Do** plan ahead to avoid unnecessary fees that can add up over time. For example, cell phone overages, parking tickets, lost or overdue library books, overdraft fees, and charges for misplaced ID cards.
- **Do** utilize your meal plan, rather than paying out of pocket for food.
- **Do** leverage your student status when student discounts are available.
- **Do** attend social events and activities on campus. This not only helps you save money, but it also increases your integration into the university and campus community.
- **Do** begin a savings account, and contribute to it on a consistent basis. This can also be linked to your checking account and serve as overdraft protection.
- **Do** use electronic resources to help manage your money.

- **Don't** try to compete with others on spending.
- **Don't** sign up for multiple credit cards. While establishing credit in college can yield positive results, if you choose to take this route, limit yourself to one credit card, and pay it ON TIME.
- **Don't** use "retail therapy" as a way of managing negative emotions or stress management.
- **Don't** use your student loans or financial aid to finance your lifestyle; use it to pay for your education!
- **Don't** use your credit card for everyday purchases; limit use for emergencies only.
- **Don't** be caught unprepared. Allow a part of your budget to account for unexpected expenses—but keep it separate from your savings.
- **Don't** forget to check your account balance regularly.
- **Don't** drive your car if you don't have to, particularly without considering costs of gas and maintenance.
- **Don't** use credit—including online purchases—when you can use cash. It's easier to spend frivolously when you delay payment.
- **Don't** spend large amounts of money on things that will decrease in value almost immediately.

Worksheet 11.1: TRACKING YOUR BUDGET

Monthly Income

Work study: _____

Part-time job: _____

Financial aid/scholarships or grants/loans: _____

Allowance from family: _____

Other sources of income: _____

Total monthly income: $_____

Monthly Expenses

Tuition and fees: _____

Textbooks and other supplies: _____

Rent/housing: _____

Transportation: _____

Utilities: _____

Food: _____

Cell phone: _____

Entertainment: _____

Credit card payments: _____

Savings: _____

Other: _____

Other: _____

Total monthly expenses: $_____

Worksheet 11.2: TRACKING YOUR WEEKLY SPENDING

The sheet below provides you with an opportunity to identify your spending habits and recognize patterns that may contribute to poor money management. For one week, keep track of every dollar you spend either in person or online using both cash and credit. No expense is too "minor" for you to track; it may be easier to use a sheet of paper that you can keep in your pocket on a daily basis, and transfer it to the worksheet at the end of the day. The resources section also includes electronic methods of tracking your spending as well (i.e. Mint.com).

Monday	Tuesday	Wednesday	Thursday
Total : _____	Total : _____	Total : _____	Total : _____
Friday	**Saturday**	**Sunday**	**TOTAL WEEKLY SPENDING:**
Total : _____	Total : _____	Total : _____	

RESOURCES

NCAA
- NCAA Eligibility Center – Guide for The College-Bound Student-Athlete

- NCAA Transfer Student Guide

- International Standards – Guide to International Academic Standards for Athletics Eligibility

- NCAA Inclusion of Transgender Student-Athletes

National Organizations
- Diversity
    - Campus Pride
    - Athlete Ally
    - Safe4Athletes
    - You Can Play

- Mental Health
    - Active Minds
    - NAMI
    - The JED Foundation

Websites
- Financial Management
    - Mint.com
    - Handsonbanking.com

- Mental Health
    - Transitionyear.org

- Diversity
    - Fearlessproject.org

REFERENCES

Al-Sharman, A., & Siengsukon, C.F. (2013). Sleep enhances learning of a functional motor task in young adults. *Physical Therapy*, 93(12), 1625-1635.

American Council on Education & American Association of University Professors, (2000). *Does diversity make a difference?* Washington, DC.

American College Health Association. (2009). American College Health Association. *National College Health Assessment II: Reference Group Executive Summary.* Linthicum, MD: Author.

Ancis, J., Sedlacek, W., & Mohr, J. (2000). Student perceptions of campus cultural climate by race. *Journal of Counseling and Development, 78(2)*, 180-185.

Ardern, C. L., Taylor, N. F., Feller, J. A., & Webster, K. E. (2013). A systematic review of the psychological factors associated with returning to sport following injury. *British Journal of Sports Medicine, 47*(17), 1120-1126.

Bacha, N. N., Bahous, R., & Nabhani, M. (2012). High Schooler's Views on Academic Integrity. *Research Papers in Education, 27*(3), 365-381.

Beanland, V., Pammer, K. (2012). Minds on the blink: The relationship between inattentional blindness and attentional blink. *Attention, Perception, & Psychophysics, 74*, 322-330.

Bird, S. P. (2013). Sleep, recovery, and athletic performance: A brief review and recommendations. *Strength & Conditioning Journal,* 35(5), 43-47.

Bowen, D., & Green, J. (2012). Does athletic success come at the expense of academic success? *Journal of Research Education, 22* (2).

Bredemeier, K., & Simons, D. J. (2012). Working memory and inattentional blindness. *Psychonomic Bulletin & Review, 19, 239-244.*

Brewer, B., Cornelius, A., Stephan, Y., & Van Raalte, J. (2010). Self-protective changes in athletic identity following anterior cruciate ligament reconstruction. *Psychology of Sport & Exercise, 11(1)*, 1-5.

Brewer, B.W., Van Raalte, J. and Linder, D. (1993). Athletic Identity: Hercules' muscles or Achilles' heel? *International Journal of Sport Psychology*, 24, 237-254.

Brown, C., Gladstetter-Fender, C., & Shelton, M. (2000). Psychosocial identity and career control in college student-athletes. Journal *of Vocational Behavior, 56(1)*, 53-62.

Bruening, J.E., Armstrong, K.L, & Pastore, D.L. (2005). Listening to the voices: The experiences of African American female student-athletes. *Research Quarterly for Exercise and Sport, 76 (1),82-100*

Burke, K., Burke, J., Regier, D., & Rae, D. (1990). Age at onset of selected mental disorders in five community populations. *JAMA Psychiatry, 47*(6), 511-518.

Burke L., Keins, B., & Ivy J., (2004). Carbohydrates and fat for training and recovery. *Journal of Sport Science, 22*, 15-30.

Burns, R., Schiller, M. R., Merrick, M. A., Wolf, K. N. (2004). Intercollegiate student athlete use of nutritional supplements and the role of athletic trainers and dietitians in nutrition counseling. *Journal of the American Dietetic Association, 104* (2), 246-249.

Cabrera, A. F., Nora, A., Terenzini, P. T., Pascarella, E. T., & Hagedorn, L. S. (1999). Campus racial climate and the adjustment of students to college: A comparison between white students and African-American students. *Journal of Higher Education, 70,* 134-160.

Center for Disease Control (2013). *Rates of TBI-related Emergency Department Visits, Hospitalizations, and Deaths — United States, 2001–2010.* Retrieved from: http://www.cdc.gov/traumaticbraininjury/data/rates.html

Chang, M. (1999). Does racial diversity matter?: The educational impact of a racially diverse undergraduate population. *Journal of College Student Development, 40*(4), 377-395.

Cheating Fact Sheet (1999). Retrieved from: http://www.glass-castle.com/clients/www-nocheating-org/adcouncil/research/cheatingfactsheet.html

Chelladurai, P., & Saleh, S.D. (1978). Preferred leadership in sports. *Canadian Journal of Applied Sport Sciences, 3,* 85–92.

Comeaux, E., (2012). Unmasking athlete microaggressions: Division I student-athletes' engagement with members of the campus community. *Journal of Intercollegiate Sport, 5*(2),189-198.

Costello, K. (2006). Why it does pay to fall asleep! *Coach & Athletic Director*, 77.

Covey, S. R. (1989). *The seven habits of highly effective people.* New York: Simon & Schuster.

Dee, T. (2014). Stereotype threat and the student-athlete. *Economic Inquiry, 52(1)*, 173-182.

Disc® classic validation report. (2008). Inscape Publishing.

Downs, M. F., & Eisenberg, D. (2012). *Journal of American College Health, 60 (2), 104-114.*

Eisenberg, D., Downs, M. F., Golberstein, E., & Zivin, K. (2009). *Medical Care Research & Review, 66* (5), 522-541.

Engstrom, C. M., & Sedlacek, W. E. (1991). A study of prejudice toward university student -athletes. *Journal of Counseling & Development, 70,* 189-193

Fleming, N., & Mills, C. (1992). Not another inventory, rather a catalyst for reflection. *To Improve the Academy, 11,* 137-155.

Frankowski, Barbara L. &Committee on Adolescence (2004). Sexual orientation and adolescents. *Pediatrics, 113*(6), 1827-1832.

Galloway, M. K. (2012). Cheating in advantaged high schools: Prevalence, justifications, and possibilities for change. *Ethics & Behavior, 22*(5), 378-399.

Giuliano, F., Migliorini, S., Benocci, R., Facchini, A., Casini, M., Corradeschi, F. (2007). Effect of mental imagery on the development of skilled motor actions. *Perceptual and Motor Skills, 105(3)*, 803-827.

Goleman, D., Boyatzis, R. E., & McKee, A., (2013). Primal leadership: Learning to lead with emotional intelligence.

Goleman, D. (1998). What makes a leader? *Harvard Business Review, Nov-Dec*, 91-102.

Griffin, P., & Hudson, T. (2013). Retrieved from http://www.ncaapublications.com/productdownloads/CRLGBTQ.pdf

Gurin P., Dey, E., Hurtado, S., & Gurin, G. (2002). Diversity and higher education: Theory and impact on educational outcomes. *Harvard Educational Review, 72*(3), 330-367.

Halstead, M. E., McAvoy, K., Devore, C. D., Carl, R., Lee, M., & Logan, K. (2013). Return ing to learning following a concussion. *Pediatrics, 132*(5), 948-957.

Hildebrand, K. M., Johnson, D. J., & Bogle, K. (2001). Comparison of patterns of alcohol use between high school and college athletes and non-athletes. *College Student Journal 35, 358–365.*

Horton, R., & Mack, D. (2000). Athletic Identity in Marathon Runners: Functional Focus or Dysfunctional Commitment? *Journal of Sport Behavior*, 23, 101-120.

Hughes, R., & Coakley, J. (1991). Positive deviance among athletes: The implications of overconformity to the sport ethic. *Sociology of Sport Journal, 8*(4), 307-325.

Humphrey, J. H., Yow, D. A. & Bowden, W. W. (2000). Stress in college athletics: Causes, consequences, coping. Binghamton, NY: The *Haworth Half-Court Press.*

Hurtado, S., Milem, J., Clayton-Pedersen, A., & Allen, W. (1998). Enacting campus climates for racial/ethnic diversity through educational policy and practice. *The Review of Higher Education, 21(3)*, 278-297.

Hurtado, S., Milem, J., Clayton-Pedersen, A., & Allen, W. (1999). Enacting diverse learning environments: Improving the climate for racial/ethnic diversity in higher education. Washington, D.C.: The George Washington University

Hylin, M. J., Orsi, S. A., Rozas, N. S., Hill, J. L., Zhao, J., Redell, J. B., Moore, A. N., & Dash, P. K. (2013). Repeated mild closed head injury impairs short-term visuospatial memory and complex learning, *Journal of Neurotrauma, 30*(9), 716-726.

Ishitani, T., & DesJardins, S. (2002). A longitudinal investigation of dropout from college in the United States. *Journal of College Student Retention: Research, Theory & Practice, 4*(2),173-201.

Jarraya, M., Jarraya, S., Chtourou, H., Souissi, N., & Chamari, K. (2013). The effect of partial sleep deprivation on the reaction time and the attentional capacities of the handball goalkeeper. *Biological Rhythm Research, 44*(3), 503-511.

Jones, K., & Harrison, Y. (2001). Frontal lobe function, sleep loss and fragmented sleep. *Sleep Medicine Reviews, 5*(6), 463-475.

Kessler. R., Berglund, P., Demler, O., Jin, R., Merikangas, K., & Walters, E. (2005). Life time prevalence and age-of-onset distributions of DSM-IV disorders in the national comorbidity survey replication. *JAMA Psychiatry, 62*(6), 593-602.

Lambert, T. A., Kahn, A. S., & Apple, K. J. (2003). Pluralistic ignorance and hooking up. *Journal of Sex Research, 40,* 129–133.

Lang, P. J. (1979). A bio-informational theory of emotional imagery. *Psychophysiology, 17,* 495-512

Laquale, K. M. (2007). Energy in-energy out: A balanced equation? *Athletic Therapy Today, 12(5),* 34-37.

Lee, J. (2002). Religion and college attendance: Change among students. *The Review of Higher Education, 25*(4), *369-384.*

Leichliter, J. S., Meilman, P. W., Presley, C. A., Cashin, J. R. (1998). Alcohol use and related consequences among students with varying levels of involvement in college athletics. *Journal of American College Health 46, 257–262.*

Leproult, R., Copinschi, G., Buxton, O., & Van Cauter, E. (1997). Sleep loss results in an elevation of cortisol levels the next evening. *Sleep, 20,* 865-870.

Leproult, R., Van Reeth, O., Byrne, M., et al. (1997). Sleepiness, performance, and neuroendocrine function during sleep deprivation: Effects of exposure to bright light or exercise. *Journal of Biological Rhythms, 12,* 245-258.

Mah, C. (2009). *Study Shows Sleep Extension Improves Athletic Performance and Mood.* Presented at the Annual Meeting of the Associated Professional Sleep Societies.

Martin, J.M. (2010). Stigma and student mental health in higher education. *Higher Education Research & Development*, 29(3), 259-274.

Martin S., Wrisberg C., & Jousbury. J. (1996). NCAA Division I athletes' perceptions of psychological skills and attitudes toward seeking sport psychology consultation, DigitalCommons @ University of Nebraska - Lincoln. 1996.

Martin, S., Wrisberg, C. A, & Lounsbury, J. W. (1996). NCAA Division I Athletes' Perceptions of Psychological Skills and Attitudes Toward Seeking Sport Psychology Consultation. *Different Perspectives on Majority Rules.* Paper 26, Retrieved from http://digitalcommons.unl.edu/pocpwi1st/26

McCarthy, K. J. (2000). The effects of student activity participation, gender, ethnicity, and socio-economic level on high school student grade point averages and attendance. Retrieved from http://www.eric.ed.gov/PDFS/ED457173.pdf

McGuire, S. P., & Belcheir, M. (2013). Transfer student characteristics matter. *Journal of College Student Retention: Research, Theory and Practice,15(1),* 37-48.

Mercincavage, J. E., & Brooks, C. I. (1990). Differences in achievement motivation of college business majors as a function of year of college and classroom seating position. *Psychological Reports, 66*(2), 632-634

Merisotis, J.P., & Phipps, R.A. (1999). What's the difference? Outcomes of distance vs. traditional classroom based learning. *Change, 31*(3), 13-17.

Miller, P. & Kerr, G. (2003). The Role Experimentation of Intercollegiate Student Athletes. *The Sport Psychologist*, 17, 196-219.

Mish, F. (2004). The Merriam-Webster dictionary . (11th ed.). Springfield, MA: Merriam-Webster.

Montello, D. R. (1988). Classroom seating location and its effect on course achievement, participation, and attitudes. *Journal of Environmental Psychology, 8(2)*, 149-157.

Mosley, M. M. (2006). The truth about high school English. In Sullivan, P., & Tinberg (Eds.). *What is "College-Level" Writing?* Urbana, Ill: National Council of Teachers of English. Available at http://wac.colostate.edu/books/collegelevel/

National Adolescent Health Information Center, University of California, San Francisco. (2007). *Fact Sheet on Reproductive Health: Adolescents and Young Adults.* Retrieved January 19, 2014, from http://nahic.ucsf.edu/downloads/ReproHlth2007.pdf

O'Connor, P. J., Lewis, R. D., & Kirschner, E. M. (1995). Eating disorder symptoms in female college gymnasts. *Medicine and Science in Sports & Exercise, 27*, 550-555.

O'Malley, P. M., & Johnson, L. D. (2002). Epidemiology of Alcohol and Other Drug Use among American College Students. *Journal of Studies on Alcohol and Drugs, Supplement No. 14:* 23-39.

Okoro, E. A. (2011). Academic integrity and student plagiarism: Guided instructional strategies for business communication assignments. *Business Communication Quarterly, 74(2)*, 173-178.

Paul, E. L., McManus, B., & Hayes, A. (2000). "Hookups": Characteristics and correlates of college students' spontaneous and anonymous sexual experiences. *Journal of Sex Research, 37, 76–88.*

Papanikolaou, Z., Nikolaidis, D., Patsiaouras, A., & Alexopoulos, P. (2003). The freshman experience: High stress-low grades. *Athletic Insight: The On-line Journal of Sport Psychology, 5.*

Pinkerton, R.S., Hinz, L.D., & Barrow, J.C. (1989). The college student-athlete: Psychological considerations and interventions. *Journal of American College Health, 37(5)*, 218-226.

Probability of Competing Beyond High School. (2013). Retrieved from http://www.ncaa.org/about/resources/research/probability-competing-beyond-high-school

Rasch, B., Buchel, C., Gais, S., & Born, J. (2007). Odor cues during slow-wave sleep prompt declarative memory consolidation. *Science, 315*, 1426-1429.

Reel, J. J., & Gill, D. L. (1996). Psychosocial factors related to eating disorders among high school and college female cheerleaders. *The Sport Psychologist, 10,* 195-206.

Rennels, M. R., & Chaudhari, R. B. (1988). Eye contact and grade distribution. *Perceptual and Motor Skills, 67(2)*, 627-632.

Reinking, M. F., & Alexander, L. E. (2005). Prevalence of Disordered-Eating Behaviors in Undergraduate Female Collegiate Athletes and Nonathletes. *Journal of Athletic Training, 40*, 47-51.

Riemer, B.A., Beal, B., & Schroeder, P. (2000). The influences of peer and university culture on female student athletes: Perceptions of career termination, professionalization, and social isolation. *Journal of Sports Behavior, 23,* 364-378.

Roland, D. (1997). The confident performer. Portsmouth, NH: Heinemann

Roval A., & Barnum, K. (2003). "On—line course effectiveness: An analysis of student interactions and perceptions of learning," *Journal of Distance Education, (18)1*, 57-73.

Sanbonmatsu D. M., Strayer D. L., Medeiros-Ward, N., & Watson, J. M. (2013). Who multi-tasks and why? Multi-tasking ability, perceived multi-tasking ability, impulsivity, and sensation seeking. *PLoS ONE, 8,* 1-8.

Sarchiapone M. et al. (2014). Hours of sleep in adolescents and its association with anxiety, emotional concerns, and suicidal ideation. *Sleep Medicine,* http://dx.doi.org/10.1016/j.sleep.2013.11.780

Sedlacek, W. E., & Adams-Gaston, J. (1992). Predicting the academic success of student-athletes using SAT and non-cognitive variables. *Journal of Counseling and Development, 70,* 724-727.

Smith, H. W. (1994). *The 10 natural laws of successful time and life management: Proven strategies for increased productivity and inner peace.* New York: Warner.

Stone, J., Harrison, C. K., & Mottley, J. (2012). "Don't call me a student-athlete: The effect of identity priming on stereotype threat for academically engaged African American college athletes. *Basic & Applied Social Psychology, 34*(2), 99-106.

Storch, E., Storch, J., Killiany, E., & Roberti, J. (2005). Self-Reported Psychopathology in Athletes: A Comparison of Intercollegiate Student-Athletes and Non-Athletes. *Journal of Sport Behavior, 28*(1), 86-97.

Strom, P. S., Strom, R. D., (2007). Cheating in Middle and High Schools. *The Educational Forum, 71(2)*, 104-116.

Sullivan, P., Tinburg, H., & Blau, S. (2010). What is college level writing? http://www.ncte.org/library/nctefiles/resources/books/sample/56766intro_chap01_x.pdf

Swail, W. S. (2004). *The art of student retention: A handbook for practioners and administrators*. Austin, TX: Educational Policy Institute.

Tinto, V. (1987). *Leaving college: Rethinking the cause and cures of student attrition*. Chicago: University of Chicago Press.

Tinto, V. (1999). Taking retention seriously: Rethinking the first year of college. *NACADA Journal, 19*(2), 5-9.

Torres-McGehee, T. M., Monsma, E. V., Gay, J. L., Minton, D. M., &, Mady-Foster, A. N. (2011). Prevalence of eating disorder risk and body image distortion among National Collegiate Athletic Association Division I varsity equestrian athletes. *Journal of Athletic Training, 46(4)*, 431-437.

Townsend, B. K., & Wilson, K. B. (2008). The academic and social integration of persisting community college transfer students. *Journal of College Student Retention: Research, Theory and Practice, 10(4)*, 405-423.

Tyrance, S. C., Harris, H. L., & Post, P. (2013). Predicting positive career planning attitudes among NCAA Division I college student-athletes. *Journal of Clinical Sport Psychology, 7(1)*, 22-40.

U.S. Department of Education, National Center for Education Statistics. (2013). *The Condition of Education 2013* (NCES 2013–037), Annual Earnings of Young Adults.

Van Dijk, S. (2011). *Don't let your emotions run your life for teens: Dialectical behavior therapy skills for helping you manage mood swings, control angry outbursts, and get along with others*. New Harbinger Publications, Inc.: Oakland, CA

Van Noordt, S., & Good, D. (2011). Mild head injury and sympathetic arousal: Investigating relationships with decision-making and neuropsychological performance in university students. *Brain Injury, 25(7)*, 707-716.

Venter, R. (2012). Role of sleep in performance and recovery of athletes: A review article. *South African Journal for Research in Sport, Physical Education & Recreation, 34 (1)*, 167-185.

Waldron, J. J., Stiles-Shipley, J. A., & Michalenok, J. J. (2001). Relationships among body satisfaction, social physique anxiety, and eating behaviors in female athletes and exercisers. *Journal of Sport Behavior, 24, 247-264.*

Warren Alfson. (2013). Retrieved from http://www.huskers.com/ViewArticle.dbml? DB_OEM_ID=100&ATCLID=944901

Watson, J. (2005). College student-athletes' attitudes toward help-seeking behavior and expectations of counseling services. *Journal of College Student Development, 46(4)*, 442-449.

Watson, J. C. & Kissinger, D. (2007). Athletic Participation and Wellness: Implications for Counseling College Student-Athletes. *Journal of College Counseling*, 10, 153-162.

Weinberg, R., & Gould, D. (2011). Foundations of Sport and Exercise Psychology (5th ed.). Human Kinetics: Champaign, IL.

Wilson , G., & Prithcard, M. (2005). Comparing sources of stress in college student athletes and non-athletes. *Athletic Insight*, 7(1), 1-8.

Woosley, S., & Shepler, D., (2011). Understanding the early integration experiences of first generation college students, *College Student Journal, 45(4)*, 700-714.

Yopyk, D. J. A., & Prentice, D. A. (2005). Am I an athlete or a student? Identity salience and stereotype threat in student-athletes. *Basic and Applied Social Psychology, 27,* 329-336.

Zaff, J. F., Moore, K. A., Papillo, A. R., & Williams, S. (2003). Implications of extracurricular activity participation during adolescence on positive outcomes. *Journal of Adolescent Research, 18,* 599-630.

Ziegler, P.J., Shoo, C.S., Sherr, B., Nelson, J. A., Larson, W.M., & Drewnowski, A. (1998). Body image and dieting behaviors among elite figure skaters. *International Journal of Eating Disorders, 24,* 421-427.

INDEX

ABOUT THE AUTHORS

Shaun Tyrance, Ph.D.

Shaun Tyrance is a licensed therapist who specializes in sport psychology. Shaun earned his Ph.D. in Counseling from the University of North Carolina at Charlotte and holds a Master's in Sport Psychology from the University of North Carolina at Greensboro. He was a four–year varsity letter winner in football at Davidson College where he played quarterback. Shaun served as an academic advisor for football at North Carolina State University, and the full-time Sport Psychology Consultant at Chip Ganassi Racing in NASCAR and the University of North Carolina at Charlotte. As a consultant, Shaun has worked with hundreds of college and professional athletes.

Nyaka NiiLampti, Ph.D.

Nyaka NiiLampti is a licensed psychologist at Southeast Psych and an Assistant Professor of Psychology at Queens University of Charlotte, where she also serves as Faculty Athletic Representative to the NCAA. She was a four-year varsity letter winner in track and field at Princeton University. She earned her Ph.D. in Counseling Psychology from Temple University, and has a Master's in Sport Psychology from the University of North Carolina-Chapel Hill. Her experiences have included teaching, clinical work, and serving in a consultative capacity in a variety of settings, including high schools, colleges and university and large sports organizations.

Winning at the College Level

CPSIA information can be obtained
at www.ICGtesting.com
Printed in the USA
LVOW03s0757300716

498140LV00001B/2/P